elegant gifts in
polymer clay

elegant gifts in *polymer* *clay*

Lisa Pavelka

NORTH LIGHT BOOKS
CINCINNATI, OHIO
www.artistsnetwork.com

about the author

Lisa Pavelka is an award-winning artist whose polymer clay expertise is recognized internationally. She has been working extensively with the medium since 1988. In addition to her first polymer clay book, *Polymer Clay Extravaganza*, Lisa has written for over a dozen magazines, including *Family Circle*, *Belle Armoire*, *Rubber Stamper* and *Crafts*. She is a columnist for *Polymer Café* magazine. Lisa appears as a regular guest on HGTV's *Carol Duvall Show* in addition to making appearances on the Discovery Channel and the DIY Network. Companies such as Dremel, Fiskars and Toner Plastics, to name a few, have sought out Lisa's expertise. Lisa volunteers her services on a regular basis to teach polymer clay workshops for children of all ages. She is president and founder of the Las Vegas Polymer Clay Guild.

Elegant Gifts in Polymer Clay. Copyright © 2004 by Lisa Pavelka. Manufactured in China. All rights reserved. The patterns and drawings in the book are for the personal use of the reader. By permission of the author and publisher, they may be either hand-traced or photocopied to make single copies, but under no circumstances may they be resold or republished. It is permissible for the purchaser to make the projects contained herein and sell them at fairs, bazaars and craft shows. No other part of this book may be reproduced in any form or by any electronic or mechanical means, including information storage and retrieval systems, without permission in writing from the publisher, except by a reviewer, who may quote a brief passage in review. Published by North Light Books, an imprint of F+W Publications, Inc., 4700 East Galbraith Road, Cincinnati, Ohio 45236. (800) 289-0963. First edition.

08 07 06 05 04   5 4 3 2 1

Library of Congress Cataloging-in-Publication Division
Elegant gifts in polymer clay / Lisa Pavelka.
     p. cm.
  Includes Index.
  ISBN 1-58180-571-3 (alk. paper)
  1. Polymer Clay Craft. I. Title.

TT297.P3297 2004
731.4'2--dc22
                    2004043358

Editor: David Oeters
Cover Designer: Stephanie Strang
Interior Designer: Terri Eubanks
Production Coordinator: Sara Dumford
Photographers: Tim Grondin, Christine Polomsky, Hal Barkan and Catherine Guillotte.

METRIC CONVERSION CHART

to convert	to	multiply by
Inches	Centimeters	2.54
Centimeters	Inches	0.4
Feet	Centimeters	30.5
Centimeters	Feet	0.03
Yards	Meters	0.9
Meters	Yards	1.1
Sq. Inches	Sq. Centimeters	6.45
Sq. Centimeters	Sq. Inches	0.16
Sq. Feet	Sq. Meters	0.09
Sq. Meters	Sq. Feet	10.8
Sq. Yards	Sq. Meters	0.8
Sq. Meters	Sq. Yards	1.2
Pounds	Kilograms	0.45
Kilograms	Pounds	2.2
Ounces	Grams	28.4
Grams	Ounces	0.04

dedication

To my children: Jeremy, Nick, Danielle and Anne, for the unbridled joy you've given me.

acknowledgments

Writing any book is a tremendous undertaking and a privilege. For me, this would have never been possible without a great deal of help and support. I would like to acknowledge the following people and companies whose generous support has helped make this book possible.

My boundless appreciation goes out to my family for their support, patience and understanding, especially to my incredible husband, Allen. Your unconditional love and support mean more to me than you will ever know. Undying gratitude to my mother, Karoline, and step-father, Howie, for their guidance and encouragement. Lastly, but never least, my brother, David, one of the funniest and most talented people I know.

Let me thank Kato Polyclay/Van Aken International, who provided all the clay used in the book. Robert, Suzanne, Tony and Amaryllis, I'm thrilled and honored to be a part of the team.

Poly clay thanks go out to too many people to name, but I absolutely must acknowledge my dear friend and mentor, Donna Kato. I could never thank her enough for everything! To the "Kato-ettes:" Judy Belcher, Kim Cavender, Gail Ritchie, Sue Kelsey, Maria Del Pinto, Cathy Johnson and Jacqueline Lee, you're the greatest!

I'd like to offer a tremendous amount of gratitude to Carol Duvall for her friendship and unswerving belief in me. To the world's greatest producers (and darn good friends) Kelly Ehrlich and Lindsey Paddor; and the rest of the *Carol Duvall Show* crew, thanks for your friendship and support.

Hugs and kisses to the most supportive friends a girl can ask for: Joy Petitclerc, "Soul Sister" Linda Steiner, Sue Sullivan and too many more to mention.

My undying gratitude goes out to my polymer clay and artist buddies. It would take a chapter to mention all of you, but I would be remiss in not mentioning the following people who have been unfailing sources of support, encouragement and inspiration—Jimm and Audrey Freedman, Gwen Gibson, KLEW (Karen Lewis), Tera Leigh, Pam Pierce, Julie Wise and Karen Thomas. Heartfelt thanks go to the ladies of the Las Vegas Polymer Clay Guild. Your support means the world to me.

A final thank-you to Hammerhead Adhesives, Hero Arts, Kemper Enterprises, Leather Factory, Memory Maker Bracelet, National Artcraft, Ranger Ink, Rio Grande, Stamp Oasis, Toner Plastics and Walnut Hollow, for generously providing many of the materials used in this book.

The biggest thanks of all go to my friends at North Light Books, especially my editor "D.J. Dave" Oeters, Christine "You Crack Me Up" Polomsky, Sally "Whyyy!!!" Finnegan and Tricia Waddell. Your support and continued belief in me mean more than you will ever know.

table
of contents

Polymer clay is so much more than a creative medium; it's a gift to those who are open to its limitless possibilities. This amazing material can be used to create, in a matter of hours, anything from breathtaking works of art to quick and easy gifts. I've witnessed the miracle that polymer clay can have on someone who has always doubted his or her creative abilities. Something magical happens when they "grab a slab" of polymer clay.

I wrote this book in the hopes of inspiring both nonclayers and polymer clay users alike. These projects are meant to be fun while still offering varying degrees of challenge. An emphasis on mixed media can be found throughout the book.

Once you've learned the techniques contained in this book, I encourage you to add your own unique variations. My wish is that regardless of your experience with polymer clay, you'll find yourself inspired to experiment. Adapting the techniques and concepts in this book will help you stretch your creative boundaries.

I'm always happy to hear from my readers. Please feel free to contact me at my Web site, www.heartinhandstudio.com.

— Happy Claying!

Lisa Pavelka

polymer clay
101

*t*his chapter covers all the polymer clay basics regarding materials, tools and safety. For those of you with more experience, this chapter can be quite helpful. Just when you think that everything has been done with the medium, something else develops. You'll find new information about polymer clay and related products in this section. Read on! You'll never know what tips and tricks lie within.

There are a variety of clays on the market. Experiment to discover which works best for you.

Polymer Clay

Many different brands of polymer clay are available throughout the world. Each has its own unique properties. Of course, the brand you use is ultimately up to you, but I'm listing the three strongest and most commonly available brands. I've also included some useful information on using clay.

Kato Polyclay

The newest of the polymer clays is named for its developer, Donna Kato. This is the strongest clay after curing and bakes with a satin finish. Kato Polyclay does not have the color-shifting problems that so frequently occur with other brands. This clay is also excellent for caning. Canes can be sliced immediately after caning with little or no distortion.

Premo Sculpey

Premo Sculpey is fairly strong after curing. It bakes with a slightly matte finish and has some flexibility after baking. It is slightly softer than Kato Polyclay for conditioning and much softer than Fimo Classic. Millefiori canes require a day or two of resting in order to be sliced without distortion.

Fimo Classic

Fimo is one of the oldest brands of polymer clay. This clay is excellent for caning; color definition remains sharp and clear. It can be difficult to condition as it often has a crumbly consistency right out of the package. Using a dedicated food processor is helpful in conditioning this clay.

Clay Storage

Polymer clay can be stored in most types of plastic—from zippered bags and recycled butter tubs to embroidery floss organizers and fishing tackle boxes. Never store polymer clay in any plastic that is crystal clear and brittle, and never leave unbaked clay on painted, varnished or lacquered surfaces. Polymer clay will react to these materials. Once baked, polymer clay is completely inert and safe to set on any surface.

While polymer clay doesn't dry out, it will attract airborne substances such as dust and pet hair. If you are working on a project and need to step away from it for some time, place a piece of plastic wrap over your work to protect it from debris.

Baking Clay

Always follow the clay manufacturer's directions for baking time and temperature. The general rule of thumb is to bake the clay 20 minutes for every ¼" (6mm) of thickness.

Using a dedicated oven to bake your clay is a good idea. If you don't have that option, make sure you wipe out your home oven with a damp sponge and baking soda after baking polymer clay. Or you can place your clay in a dedicated roasting pan with a lid. If your clay project is too tall to bake with the lid on, tent the roaster with aluminum foil.

Liquid Polymer Clay

As a relatively new product, liquid polymer clay's applications have only just begun to be explored. This product makes an excellent sealant for surface treatments such as metallic leafing, foil and image transfers. It's ideal for seating polymer clay mosaics or for use as an adhesive. Liquid polymer clay can also be used to laminate or transfer images. It may be added to stiff clay as an emulsifier to help in conditioning. Liquid polymer clay can also be turned into a surface treatment by adding dyes, pigments, acrylic paint, mica powders and glitter. Let your imagination run wild and have fun playing with this exciting product.

Liquid polymer clay

Brushes used with liquid polymer clay must remain dedicated to use with the medium. To care for these brushes, wipe off excess clay after each use. Store the brushes handle-down. Cover the bristles with the corner of a plastic bag. Occasionally, liquid polymer clay brushes get rather "chunky." Clean the brush by placing a few drops of liquid polymer clay onto the bristles. Carefully work the clay into the bristles with a toothpick to loosen the gunk.

Kato Clear Polyclay Medium

This brand is the thinnest and most translucent of the liquid clays. It bakes with a satiny shine. It can be polished to a glasslike finish with 600-grit wet/dry sandpaper, followed by buffing.

Translucent Liquid Sculpey

This clay is thicker than Kato liquid clay. It can be thinned with Sculpey Clay Softener. This clay bakes with a milky finish that can be made more translucent by sanding and polishing.

Baking Liquid Clay

The rule of thumb for baking liquid polymer clay is a minimum of 30 minutes in an oven, or it can be cured with a heat gun. Heat guns usually run hotter than 275° F (135° C). Care should be used to avoid burning the clay. Never hold the gun closer than 6" (15cm) from the clay and always keep the gun moving back and forth. Holding it over one area too long can cause discoloration or burning.

Fusing Clay

Liquid polymer clay can be used to fuse clay to clay. Liquid clay is quite thin, and won't tack until baking. It will work by itself as an adhesive only when applying it between two flat, horizontal surfaces. For creating a permanent bond between two pieces of clay on a curved or vertical surface, place a small amount of adhesive, such as superglue or polymer clay bonder, on the center of one of the pieces to be bonded. Apply a thin ring of liquid polymer clay around the bonder. This will create the strongest fusion between clay pieces during baking.

basic
polymer clay kit

*Y*ou'll need what I call a "Basic Clay Kit" for crafting in polymer clay. It's a good idea to have these materials on hand when you are working on any polymer clay project. I've also included some information on getting the most out of some of the tools on this list. Most of these tools should be fairly easy to find on the Internet or at your local craft store, or use the resource guide at the back of the book.

The basic polymer clay kit.

Pasta Machine

A pasta machine is the most important tool for the polymer clay artist. They can be found in most housewares stores and can be ordered from several online resources such as www.appliances.com. The pasta machine has numerous uses, from conditioning clay to creating special effects like the Skinner blend.

Not all pasta machines are created equal. I recommend using only ones marked Atlas or Marcato. The dial on the side indicates the width between rollers. Since the width settings vary from machine to machine (even among machines of the same brand) the settings specified in the projects are more of a suggestion rather than a hard and fast rule.

Clay Blades

Several types of polymer clay blades are available, such as rigid and flexible blades in many different lengths. It takes some practice to figure out which blade you prefer for various types of techniques. It's good to have at least the basic T-blade and experiment with the other blades to find out what works for you. Wavy blades are excellent for creating special mokumé gané and ripple effects in clay.

To clean and sharpen the blade, fold a piece of 600-grit or 800-grit wet/dry sandpaper in half. Sandwich the sandpaper between a thick piece of fabric or sponge. Carefully run the folded sandpaper up and down both sides of the blade. This should be done with all new blades to remove the coating applied to them during manufacturing.

Automotive Protectant Spray

Automotive protectant sprays, such as Son-Of-a-Gun or Armor All, work to keep polymer clay from sticking to surfaces, allowing you to use more pressure on the clay without having it stick to the acrylic rod. Some people use cornstarch or talcum powder as a release agent for stamps and texture sheets. These can leave a residue which can be washed away, but also leaves a barely discernible texture in the clay. It is for this reason I prefer silicone-based automotive protectant spray as a release agent.

basic clay kit

Pasta machine
8" x 8" (20cm x 20cm) or larger ceramic tiles
Clay blade
Craft knife
Acrylic clay rod/roller

Needle tool
Polymer clay bonder
Two-part epoxy
Index cards
Toothpicks

Automotive protectant spray
Waxed deli sheets
Tweezers
Ruler

Polymer Clay Bonder

Polymer clay bonder is a cyanoacrylate adhesive, or superglue, that has been specially formulated for use at high temperatures. The adhesive bond of ordinary superglues breaks down during the curing process. Polymer clay bonder adheres raw clays together in seconds and can attach raw clay to cured clay. Bonder is used in most projects of this book and is considered a temporary fusing agent.

Two-Part Epoxy

Two-part epoxy is the strongest of glues. It works with polymer clay before and after baking. It can also be used as a sealant or a varnish. Using two-part epoxy isn't as difficult as most people think. Mix equal parts of a resin and an accelerator together on an index card with a toothpick. The glue begins setting as soon as mixing begins. Epoxies should be allowed to cure 24 hours for optimal bonding. Two-part epoxies are stronger than one-part epoxies, and are packaged in a double-barreled syringe, tube or bottles. Epoxy is a permanent adhesive. Use it for clay projects with pieces that need to be adhered together.

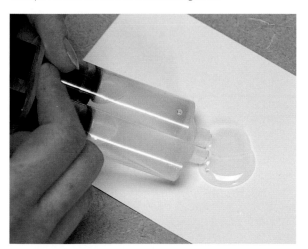

Mix two-part epoxy on an index card before using.

CARE AND FEEDING OF YOUR PASTA MACHINE

Clay residue builds up along the pasta machine rollers over time. You can periodically clean your machine by running a baby wipe through the rollers and along the guide blades underneath the rollers. Some residue buildup can be cleaned only by taking the machine apart. Never use anything with a hard, sharp point to remove the residue clay as it can scratch your rollers.

Another common problem is black streaking that occasionally appears on the clay. This streaking comes from an internal lubricant on the rollers. It is an unavoidable problem, although keeping your machine as clean as possible helps. A clay scraper designed for ceramics can shave off the top layer of clay that has been streaked.

A pasta machine should never be immersed in water. Internal components can rust, even on pasta machines labeled stainless steel. Pasta machines used with clay cannot be washed clean of clay residue. They should remain dedicated exclusively for clay use only.

tip Epoxies should be used in well-ventilated areas only. Wearing latex gloves may also be helpful when mixing and applying epoxy.

working
with clay

*t*he first step to creating exciting and beautiful polymer clay projects is knowing how to get the most from your clay. Don't worry, even if this is your first time working with clay, you'll be using it like a pro in no time!

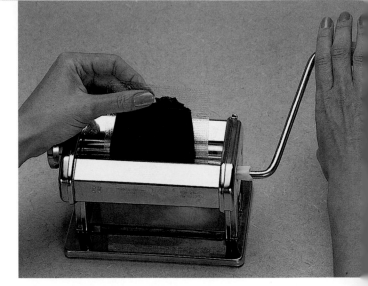

Condition the clay before you begin a project.

Properties of Clay

Polymer clay must always be conditioned before use! Skipping this step or failing to condition clay thoroughly can mean cured clay that's brittle in some areas while strong in others. It can also result in cracking during baking.

The first method of conditioning polymer clay is to knead the clay by hand for several minutes until it is soft and pliable. The second, easier option is to use a pasta machine. Cracking along the edges indicates that the clay is not thoroughly conditioned. Adding a few drops of liquid polymer clay can soften the clay, making it easier to condition. Do not add too much at a time. This can make the clay gummy and difficult to work with.

To condition crumbling clay, chop it into fine pieces, add a few drops of liquid polymer clay and place the chunks into a clay-dedicated food processor or chopper. Chop the clay for a minute or two and then compress the small, warm pieces in your palm. Hand-flatten the compressed ball of clay until it is thin enough to roll through a pasta machine on the largest setting.

If you are working with crumbly clay that doesn't respond to conditioning, it may mean that the clay has started to cure due to improper storing or premature exposure to high temperatures.

For keeping clay soft or when working in a cold room, fill half of a large plastic bag with uncooked rice or barley. Heat it in a microwave oven for about a minute. Place the clay on a deli sheet and set them both on the warm bag. This will keep the clay warm and pliable. Since microwave ovens vary, you may need to adjust your microwave time up or down to ensure the rice or barley does not become too warm. This can prematurely cure your clay.

tip

Working Properties of Clay

Factors such as the brand of clay, room temperature, work surface and hand temperature can all affect the amount of time you can work with clay before you need to recondition it. If you work in a cold room or have cold hands, you may need to recondition clay sheets more often. Clay doesn't actually dry out since it contains no water. Some brands tend to become overly soft and mushy when being worked with for extended periods. If this occurs, let it rest or place it in a plastic bag and refrigerate for a few minutes

Never place uncured clay on crystal clear plastic or anything painted, varnished or stained. It may react to the finish on furniture and certain plastics.

If your clay becomes too soft, you can stiffen it by a process called "leaching." To do this, roll out sheets of the clay and sandwich them between several layers of paper. Set the sandwiched clay over a ceramic tile and put a heavy object over the paper-covered tile. Allow the clay to sit for a day or two, then remove the paper. It will appear greasy. That's because the paper has absorbed some of the plasticizer, making the clay stiffer. A word of caution, leaching removes heat stabilizers from the clay, and can cause the clay to color shift, or change color, or scorch during baking. Leaching also reduces the strength of baked clay.

You don't have to throw away unconditionable clay. Add fine bits of partially cured clay to a contrasting color of soft clay to create the look and texture of stone.

tip

Use denim jeans to polish your projects for an elegant finish.

Use a circle cutter to make sure the ratios of a color formula are precise.

Polishing

It's simple to add an elegant satiny finish or a stunning glasslike finish on baked polymer clay. For Kato clay, sand the baked clay in water using 600-grit wet/dry sandpaper. Sand until the clay feels as smooth as it's going to get before advancing to a finer grit. For other brands of clay, sand with 600-, 800-, 1,000- and finally, 1,500-grit sandpapers.

Buff the sanded clay with a loosely woven muslin wheel attached to a jeweler's wheel, bench grinder or a drill. If one of these devices isn't available, rub the clay vigorously with a piece of old denim or 100 percent cotton cloth. For a high-gloss finish, brush on a layer of Future floor polish, which can be found in the grocery store.

Burnishing

To transfer foil (not metal leaf) onto clay, lay the foil faceup on a clay surface. Rub the foil on the clay to transfer the foil design. It's important to generate a lot of friction and heat since this is what causes the foil to adhere to the clay. Firm, even pressure should be applied, but not so much that you gouge the clay. Immediately after burnishing, lift one corner of the foil and pull the backing away very quickly! See page 18 for more information on burnishing.

Blending

Polymer clay colors can be combined to make new colors by simply mixing two or more colors together until they merge into one color. Blend colors by hand-kneading or rolling the clay through a pasta machine. Stopping short of completing this process will create a beautiful marbled effect.

Measuring Clay

Within this book you'll find projects calling for color formulas. Formulas require the mixing of clay in various ratios. An easy way to measure equal ratios of clay is to start by rolling out all colors through the largest setting of the pasta machine. Cut out the number of sections called for from each color using the same size and shape cutter and blend them together.

Cleanup

Polymer clay leaves a waxy residue on your hands. Baby wipes work well to clean hands between colors. When you're done with the clay for the day or taking a break to eat, rub a dollop of pumice-based, waterless hand cleaner thoroughly over your hands. Wash away the cleaner with soap and water to completely remove the residue.

Add a few drops of dishwashing soap to your sanding water. This is an anti-surfactant that makes sanding easier and helps the sandpaper last longer. Several pieces of sandpaper may be needed for polishing large pieces.

tip

Skinner
blending

Skinner blending is a method for creating color gradients between two or more colors. Polymer clay pioneer Judith Skinner came up with this simple, but ingenious technique. The following instructions are for the two-color Skinner blend used in several projects throughout the book.

1 Cut a 3½" x 3½" (9cm x 9cm) template from an index card. Use the template to cut out two squares of contrasting colored clays from sheets rolled through the largest setting of the pasta machine. Cut each square diagonally with the clay blade. For a more dramatic effect, offset the diagonal cut ⅛" (3mm) from each opposing corner. This will leave some of each original color in the center and outer layers of the Skinner blend cane. For a more subtle effect, make the diagonal cuts from corner to corner.

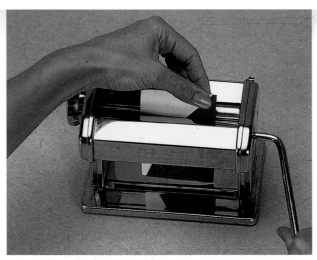

2 Stack the same color triangles, one over the other, to create a double layer of clay. Press the triangles together to form a square. Run the two-toned clay square through the pasta machine on the largest setting.

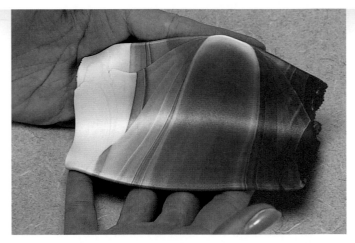

3 Fold the flattened rectangle in half and run it through the largest setting of the machine. Repeat this step 25–30 times until a smooth color gradient appears. The key to doing this technique correctly is to fold the rectangle each time so that the colors match each other on the sides. For example, white will always be folded over to white and magenta will always be folded over to magenta.

tip   Premo Sculpey is stickier than other clays and should not be allowed to fold over on itself when fed through the thinner settings of the pasta machine. The clay may tear when it's pulled apart. If working with Premo, feed the clay out onto the work surface with each pass.

4 Now it's time to stretch the gradient sheet. It's easier to work with a short, wide cane rather than a longer, narrower one. Create this by trimming the uneven sides of the sheet. Cut the sheet in half lengthwise and stack one half over the other to create a sheet of double thickness.

5 Roll this sheet lengthwise through the largest setting of the pasta machine. Continue running the sheet through the pasta machine, setting the rollers to the next smaller thickness with each pass until you have rolled the sheet through the fifth largest setting. As you continue rolling, the clay will spread until it reaches the width of the pasta machine. Because of this, it is important to start with a sufficient amount of clay when making a Skinner blend. Starting with too little clay will make it difficult to fold the clay.

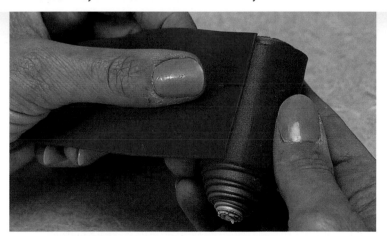

6 For the projects in this book, trim a straight edge along the lighter colored end. Roll this end, jelly roll style, toward the darker colored end of the sheet. Be sure to roll the cane tightly. Air pockets can create distortion.

7 Trim a straight edge at the end of the darker colored clay. If the darker color doesn't wrap all the way around the cane, roll a sheet of the same color through the fifth largest setting of the pasta machine. Trim it to the width of the cane and cut a straight edge along one side. Place this sheet against the end of the outer roll of the cane. Continue wrapping the sheet around until the colors match identically. Trim and remove excess clay.

tip Roll a piece of the interior colored clay into a thin snake. Place it at the end of the sheet. Roll the end of the stretched clay sheet over the snake to make it easier to begin the rolling process.

thinking outside
the clay kit

*P*olymer clay begs to be experimented with. Rather than a scientific approach, the medium lends itself more to discovery through play. Whether you experiment with the projects you find within this book or with other polymer clay projects, I encourage you to "color" outside the lines.

One of the more enjoyable ways of discovering new tools and textures to work with is to stroll the aisles of your local hardware or home-improvement store. You'll be amazed at the variety of objects you can use to help you form, texture and cover clay.

Look for ways to create interesting patterns and surface textures in polymer clay. Polymer clay can be baked with many substances including paper, cardboard, wood, papier-mâché, cornstarch packing peanuts, glass, foil, fabric, metal, feathers and so much more. Be careful not to bake clay with Styrofoam, crystal clear plastic, or plastic beads. Try your hand at making variations in the surfaces of your work. You'll be surprised where your playfulness takes you!

I've included a few of my own tricks below for getting you started thinking outside your clay kit.

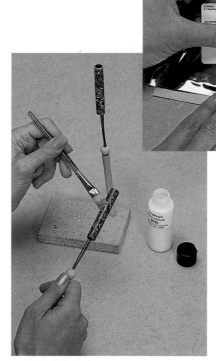

A plastic card can help you get the most out of your burnishing.

Polishing

When polishing or glazing objects like pen barrels or beads, tension rods made for decorating eggs work quite well. The tools come in various sizes and can be ordered with stands, making it possible to polish and finish clay projects without touching them.

Burnishing

An old credit card can be an invaluable tool for getting the most out of your burnishing and foil transfer techniques. Burnish for about a minute with a stiff plastic card (like a credit card). Run the card quickly over the surface, changing directions often. Make sure you use even pressure when you burnish with the card, or you could gouge the clay or damage your project.

Small speckles of clay may show through the foil left on the clay. This is normal and you shouldn't expect to lay down a solid sheet of foil. If large sections of clay show through, lay the Mylar backing over the clay again so that the remaining foil is aligned over the blank spots left on the clay. Reburnish a small area at a time, removing the backing as before.

If the foil is being stubborn and won't stick to an area after reburnishing, press your finger over the foil spot being reburnished for 10–15 seconds and quickly tear away the Mylar backing. This usually does the trick. If the foil is still not adhering, burnish a fresh piece of foil over the spot. Sometimes a clay residue builds up on the underside of the foil, making it hard to create adhesion.

Tension rods make polishing easy.

Clay Blades

Clay blades are so sharp they can be dangerous, but a few simple tricks can help you handle your clay blades safely. Create a blade trough from junk clay. Form and bake a U-shaped holder to store blades in when not in use. This will protect the sharp side of the blade, and you'll pick up the blade from the dull side. You can also store blades in a plastic toothbrush holder when you travel.

Pasta Machines

Pasta machine handles are notorious for falling out and onto your foot! Wrapping some plastic wrap or the fingertip of a latex glove over the handle end before inserting it into the machine helps prevent this from happening.

Replace the pasta machine clamp with a heavy-duty C-clamp, obtainable from any hardware store. The handle on the pasta machine clamp can easily break, and the clamp doesn't fit over many tables. A C-clamp is your best bet for attaching your machine to any work surface.

Clay Guns

The softer the clay is, the easier it is to extrude. It can still be difficult to extrude by hand. To make this process easier, wedge the plunger handle and finger grips between the open jaws of a bench vise. Crank the jaws together and watch the clay come rushing out. If the plunger starts bending, loosen the bench vise jaws and flip it over before continuing. Several products are made to aid in clay gun extrusion. See the resource guide at the back of the book for companies that carry clay accessories.

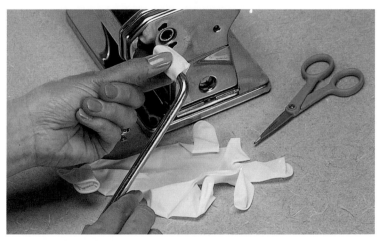

A latex glove can make using the pasta machine much easier!

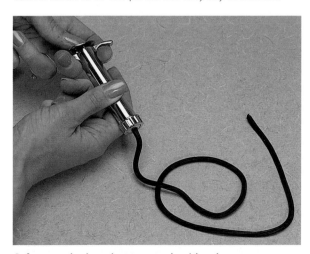

Soft, warm clay is easiest to extrude with a clay gun.

POLYMER CLAY GUILDS

A guild is a wonderful place to learn more about polymer clay. Contact the National Polymer Clay Guild (www.npcg.org) to find out if there is a guild in your area.

Guilds differ greatly around the world. They can be as small as a few friends or as large as several hundred members. Most guilds host periodic demonstrations and workshops, along with monthly meetings and clay days. If there isn't a guild in your area, you may consider starting one of your own. All you need is a friend who shares your interest in polymer clay.

Many guilds choose to give something back to the community through outreach programs that educate the public about polymer clay. A guild may adopt a charitable cause to raise money for through shows or classes. Best of all, a guild is a wonderful place to make new friends who share your love of clay.

his & her *gifts*

*l*ooking for the perfect gift for the person who has everything? Look no further! Here are five gifts that are not only unique but extremely practical. You'll take pride in knowing your gift will not only be appreciated, but put to good use. Making these gifts with your hands as well as your heart will ensure they're one-of-a-kind treasures. Achieve professional-quality finishing by following the easy step-by-step foiling, millefiori and mokumé gané techniques.

projects

mokumé gané
pen

*W*hat better gift to give the men in your life than something that is not only striking and stylish, but functional? Mokumé gané (translated "wood eye metal") was invented by master metalsmith Denbei Shoami in Japan during the seventeenth century. The technique was originally used in the making of swords. It now lends itself beautifully to polymer clay. No two pens will look alike when you use this amazing technique. A spiked furniture cup, used to protect carpet, makes a unique tool with which you'll create this pen.

Polymer clay: black, copper, silver and gold

Polaris pen kit, gold or silver (Penn State Industries #PKPOLPEN)

Spiked furniture cup (or a device with deep spikes)

Penn State pen press (optional, see sidebar page 29)

Basic clay kit

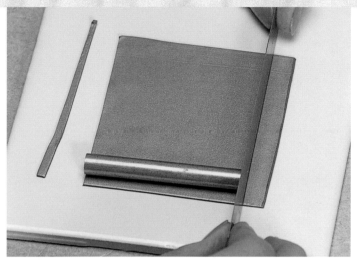

1 Roll out a sheet of silver clay on the fifth largest setting of the pasta machine. Trim the sheet to the width of the pen barrel and cut a straight edge along one side, parallel with the barrel.

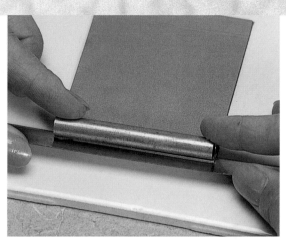

2 Use the clay blade to lift the clay up and onto the pen barrel.

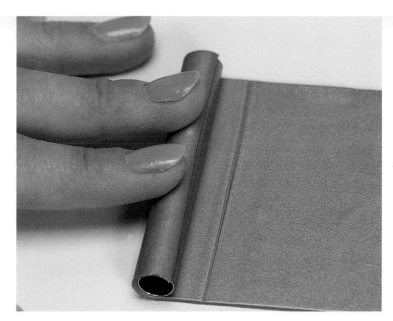

3 Roll the clay around the barrel until it overlaps onto the clay sheet, then pull the clay back. This will leave a straight line marked into the clay. Cut just inside the mark with the clay blade. Roll the pen barrel over the trimmed clay. The ends should meet up exactly. If the ends do not meet, gently stretch the clay until the edges touch. If the clay overlaps, trim the excess clay and realign the edges.

4 Smooth the seam with your fingers and roll the barrel over the work tile with the palm of your hand to heal the seam.

You can easily find furniture cups at your local home-improvement or hardware store. These are plastic with spiked tips, and are used to prevent furniture from damaging carpet.

tip

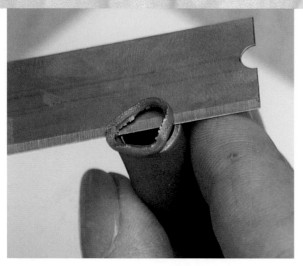

5 Trim the excess clay away from the ends of the barrel, using the clay blade.

6 Roll out two 3" x 3" (8cm x 8cm) sheets of each color on the fourth largest setting of the pasta machine. Tear all but one black sheet of clay into pieces. Place these pieces at random over the remaining black sheet of clay, building up several layers.

7 Form and compress the layers of clay into a stack with your hands.

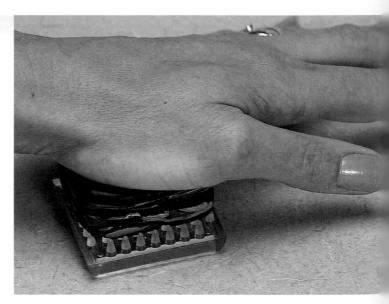

8 Press one side, then turn the clay over and press the other side of the clay stack onto the spikes of the furniture cup.

When cutting slices from the clay block, it may be necessary to occasionally reimpress it with the furniture cup to maintain the pattern.

tip

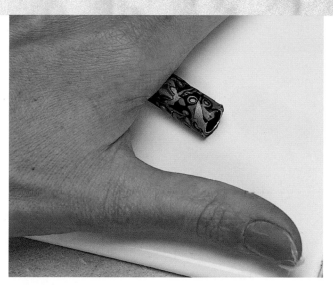

9 Slice several thin layers from the mokumé gané block and place them randomly over the clay-covered pen barrel. The base color will show through the holes and along the edges of the cane slices.

10 Roll the barrel against the work tile with the palm of your hand until all the slices are seamlessly embedded into the silver clay. Bake the barrel at 275° F (135° C) for 30 minutes.

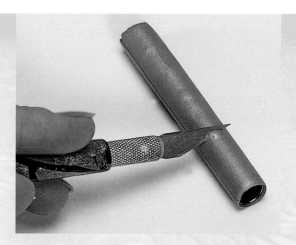

11 When the baked barrel has cooled, sand the pen in water, and then polish the pen. When finished, you may glaze the pen with floor polish. Then assemble the pen by hand or with a pen press assembly tool, following the instructions included with the kit. See page 29 for more information on pen assembly.

REMOVING AIR POCKETS

If air bubbles appear in the clay before baking, pierce them with the tip of the craft knife or needle tool. Press the air out of the slit and heal the clay back together with your fingertip before baking.

rose cane
pen

*t*here's nothing like holding a fine writing implement in your hand. You'll have not only the satisfaction of holding a precision tool when you're jotting something down, but the satisfaction of knowing you created it. You'll be surprised at how easy it is to make this unique pen embellished with a delicate millefiori rose pattern. This slimline pen is absolutely gorgeous and is easily refillable. Don't be surprised if you can't make just one!

materials

Polymer clay: pearl, magenta and green

Silver slim-line pen kit (Penn State Industries # PK-PENSAT)

Basic clay kit

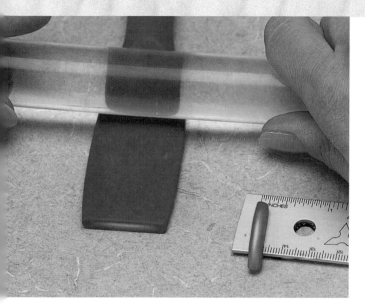

1 Create two Skinner blend canes using magenta to pearl and green to pearl clays (see page 16 for information on Skinner blend canes). Flatten the magenta/pearl cane to 1/8" (3mm) thick with the acrylic rod.

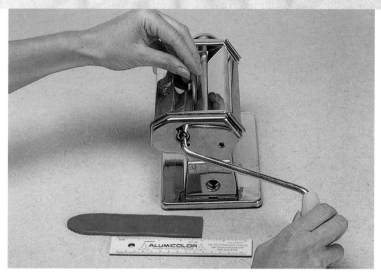

2 Cut six 1" (25mm) long sections from the flattened cane. Roll one section through the largest setting of the pasta machine. Make sure you roll the cane through widthwise.

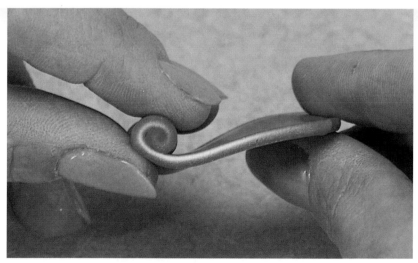

3 Roll one flattened section like a jelly roll to form the rose center.

To give your roses some variety, use a few more or a few less 1" (25mm) sections of flattened cane. More sections will give you a larger rose. Fewer sections will create more of a rosebud effect.

tip

4 Wrap the remaining five sections around the jelly roll cane, staggering their placement to form the outer petals. Cut this cane in half. Reduce one half of the cane to ¼" (6mm) in diameter (see sidebar page 29). Save the other half for more pens or another application.

5 Reduce and roll a 2" (5cm) green/pearl Skinner blend cane to 7" (18cm) long. Trim distorted ends and cut the cane into five 1" (25mm) long sections. Press four sections into a square formation, placing the fifth section in the middle at the top.

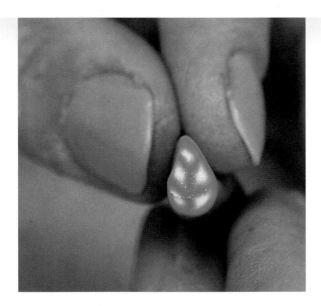

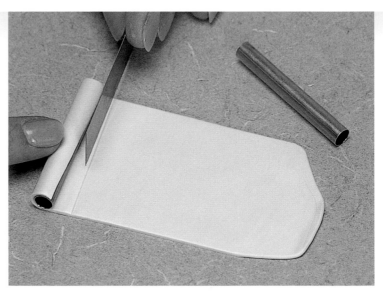

6 Compress, roll and reduce the cane to ¼" (6mm) in diameter. With the fifth cane section sitting at the top of the cane, pinch the cane into a teardrop shape.

7 Wrap both brass pen barrels with pearl clay rolled out on the fifth largest setting of the pasta machine. Trim the clay from the ends of the barrel. See steps 1–5 on pages 23–24 for directions on wrapping pen barrels with clay.

8 Cut several thin slices from the rose and leaf canes. Apply them randomly over the clay-covered barrels.

9 Roll each barrel until the cane slices blend completely into the pearl clay. There should be no visible seams between the cane slices and the pearl clay. Trim the excess clay from the barrel ends with the craft knife and bake them on an index card at 275° F (135° C) for 30 minutes. When the baked barrels are cool, you may sand, polish and glaze the barrels if you want. See page 15 for information on polishing clay. Assemble the pen following the instructions included with the kit.

REDUCING CANES

Compress a cane by squeezing and rotating it with your fingers, starting from the center and working your way out to both ends. This will remove trapped air and reduce the cane. It's essential to compress any air out of the cane when starting a reduction, or severe distortion can occur. Continue to reduce the cane by stretching and rolling for round canes. For square and triangular canes, use the acrylic rod to shape and reduce. Stretching and finger shaping can also be used or combined with the rod.

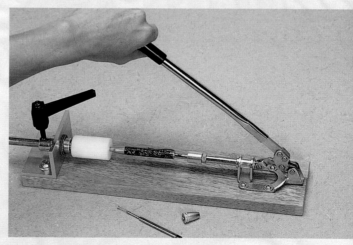

PEN PRESS

Kit pens can be assembled by hand, but it's easier and faster to use an assembly press such as this one from Penn State Industries, especially if you're going to make lots of pens. One cane or mokumé gané block should have enough clay to make several pens.

patterned foil
compact

*d*o you love the look of dichroic glass? You can create a beautiful, mirrored compact that has the look of dichroic glass with this faux technique. Even better, you can control the dichroic effect by laying it down in a pattern! Learn to create a truly glasslike effect without all the fuss and muss of polishing the clay.

materials

Polymer clay: black and white

Silver heart compact

3" × 3" (8cm × 8cm) of oil swirl polymer clay foil

Clear UTEE
(Ultra Thick Embossing Powder)

Victorian Lace texture stamp
(Heart in Hand Studio #LP-VS1)

Plastic spoon

Basic clay kit

1 Roll out a 3" x 3" (8cm x 8cm) piece of black polymer clay on the largest setting of the pasta machine. Place a 3" x 3" (8cm x 8cm) square of oil swirl polymer clay foil faceup on the black clay sheet. Burnish the foil onto the clay.

2 Place the foiled clay facedown over the texture stamp. Spray the back of the clay with automotive protectant spray and spread it over the surface with your fingertips. Roll an acrylic rod firmly over the clay in one direction only. This must be done in a single pass. Rolling the rod back and forth will distort the pattern.

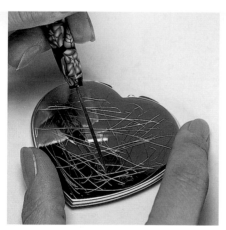

4 Deeply gouge the surface of the compact with the tip of the needle tool. This increases the adhesion of the epoxy.

3 Lift the clay from the stamp. Use a clean, sharp clay blade to shave off a very thin layer of the raised foiled clay, leaving the foil only on the embedded areas of the clay. Shave only small areas at a time. Shave as closely as possible to the foil pattern without cutting into it. It's better to shave an area repeatedly than to cut too deeply the first time and remove the foiled pattern. Carefully remove any remaining foil or clay shavings from the clay sheet, using the tip of the craft knife. If any shavings are left behind, they may be picked up on the roller and relaid on the clay, contaminating the pattern. When you're finished shaving, roll an acrylic rod over the foiled clay to smooth and flatten it.

tip

The deeper the impression made in the clay in step 2, the easier step 3 will be. Standing up while embossing will give you more leverage, allowing more pressure to be applied to the clay.

5 Apply a small drop of polymer clay bonder to the center of the compact. Lay the foiled clay over the glued surface. Working from the center, smooth out any trapped air with your fingertips. Turn the clay-covered compact facedown over a waxed deli sheet. Trim excess clay from around the compact edges with a craft knife. Turn the compact over and trim away ⅛" (3mm) of foiled clay from around the compact's edges leaving an exposed metal border.

6 Create a dam around the foiled clay by rolling out a 10" (25cm) black clay snake, ⅛" (3mm) in diameter. Attach the snake around the edge of the foiled clay using polymer clay bonder, gluing only 1"–2" (3cm–5cm) at a time, as the glue dries quickly. Trim excess clay away and blend the seam together with your fingertips.

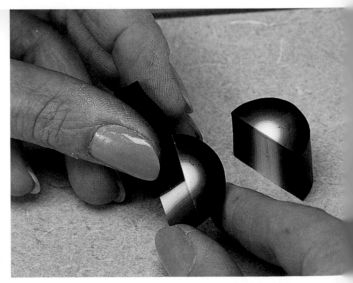

7 Use a plastic spoon to add UTEE powder to the center of the foiled clay. Spread it out toward the edges until the clay is no longer visible. Level the powder with the back of the spoon. It shouldn't sit any higher than the dam walls. Place the compact on an index card over a ceramic baking tile. Bake at 275° F (135° C) for 20 minutes or until the embossing powder melts. If you use a convection oven, make sure to cover the compact to prevent air from blowing the powder off the clay. When removing the compact from the oven, hold the tile level since the melted embossing powder remains liquid while still hot.

8 Cut a 1" (25mm) section from a black and white Skinner blend cane. Stand the cane upright and cut the cane in half, slicing down through the middle. Roll out a small sheet of black clay on the sixth largest setting of the pasta machine. Cut a straight end along one side of this sheet and trim to match the width of the cane. Lay the trimmed sheet halfway into the white center of the halved cane. Reassemble the cane halves and wrap with a layer of black clay rolled through the sixth largest setting of the pasta machine.

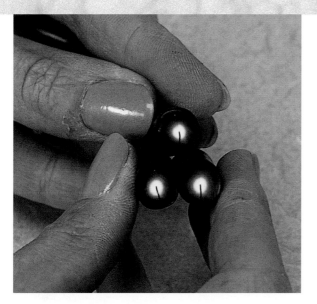

9 Reduce the cane to 4" (10cm) long. Trim the distorted ends and cut the cane into three equal pieces. Stack the three cane sections into a triangle formation. One single cane section should be placed over two cane sections, sitting side by side. All the "veins" should be pointing up from the bottom of each cane.

10 Gently compress these canes together with your fingers. Roll and reduce the compressed cane to ³⁄₈" (10mm) in diameter. Trim the distorted ends and cut off a 2" (5cm) section. Pinch the cane into a leaf shape.

11 Cut several dozen thin cane slices with the clay blade. Starting at the top-center of the compact, use polymer clay bonder to glue slices over the clay's edges along one side. Lay the slices scallop fashion (tip over end). Repeat this step on the other side until the slices meet at the bottom of the compact. If the ending slices don't meet exactly, glue a slice over the top and bottom of the heart. Bake the compact at 275º F (135º C) for 20 minutes. Remove the hot compact from the oven with care since the UTEE will have re-melted. When cool, use a fingernail or cuticle stick to carefully remove any embossing powder that may have seeped through the clay border. Carefully slide a clay blade between the clay and the heart compact to remove the clay. Reattach the clay to the compact with two-part epoxy.

faux tortoiseshell
change caddy

*C*rafting a great gift for a gentleman can be a challenge. Here's the perfect gift for organizing spare change, watches, cuff links and the like. Highly prized for its mottled elegance, tortoiseshell was widely used in the nineteenth and early twentieth centuries to create jewelry, plates and fashion accessories. The faux tortoiseshell cane you'll learn to make with clay will fool the eye with its appearance and texture. Rich, earthy colors accent a project that makes a great stand-alone décor item.

materials

Polymer clay: brown, beige, gold, ecru and 2 blocks of black (directions for making ecru clay can be found below)

7"–8" (18cm–20cm) diameter clear glass plate or pillar candleholder

1½" (4cm) circle cutter

Tracing paper

Large ball-tip stylus

Basic clay kit

1 After conditioning, chop ½ block of each color of clay (except the black clay) into small pieces. Chop ⅛ block of black into pieces. Mix all the chopped clay colors on your work surface. Tightly compact the clay chunks together with your hands. Begin kneading the ball with your hands, once the pieces are compressed. Roll or stretch the ball of clay and fold a few times. Do not overmix and blend the colors together.

2 Recompress the clay into a short, wide snake about 3" (8cm) long. Trim the ends with the clay blade. Wrap the clay snake in a black clay sheet that's been rolled through the third largest setting of the pasta machine.

3 Roll and reduce the wrapped snake to 12" (30cm) long. Trim away the distorted ends. Cut the snake into five 2" (5cm) long sections. Slightly flatten each section between your fingers. Assemble the five sections into an H formation. Tightly compact the H into a square cane using your fingers or the acrylic rod.

MAKING ECRU CLAY

Tony Aquino's color formula for making ecru clay: 4 parts white, 2 parts brown and 1½ parts yellow. For this project we are using a 1½" (4cm) circle cutter to mix the ecru formula. See page 15 for tips on mixing color formulas.

4 Shape the square cane into a triangle by pinching the entire length between your fingers. Use your fingers or an acrylic rod to stretch and reduce this cane to 7" (18cm) long. Cut away the distorted ends. Cut the trimmed cane into three 2" (5cm) sections. Assemble the three sections, side by side (with the pinched ends aligned together) to form a semicircular cane.

<big>tip</big> To help maintain the square shape of a cane cutting, flip the cane one-quarter turn after each slice. To cut thin, even slices when cutting canes, look down directly over the top edge of the clay blade to make sure you are holding it straight.

5 Cut the semicircular cane in half and assemble the two halves together. Compress the two halves together with your fingers. Reshape the cane into a square using the acrylic rod. Reduce the cane by rolling the rod over each side with several passes. Rotate the cane frequently to maintain the square shape. Continue shaping and reducing with the rod until the cane is a ¾" (19mm) square.

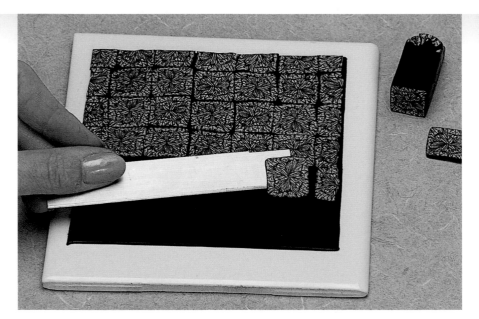

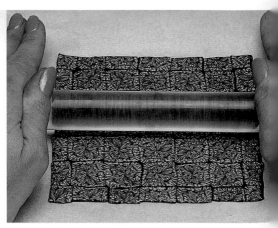

7 Roll the slices into the clay sheet with the acrylic rod. With the clay still on the waxed deli sheet, rotate the clay often to ensure the slices don't stretch too much in one direction.

6 Roll out two 5" x 5" (13cm x 13cm) sheets of black clay on the fourth largest setting of the pasta machine. Cut one edge of each sheet at a 45° angle, using the clay blade. Assemble the sheets together along the cut edges, layering one edge over the other to form one large sheet. Blend the seam with your finger. Cut several dozen thin slices, about ¹⁄₁₆" (2mm) thick, from the tortoiseshell cane with the clay blade. Cover the black clay sheet with the slices. Place the cane covered sheet onto waxed paper when you finish.

8 Once the clay looks like one solid sheet, with no visible seams between the slices, peel away the waxed paper. Gently stretch the clay sheet by pulling slightly on the ends. Rotate the sheet while stretching. Do not overstretch, as this can tear the clay sheet. Stretching will cause small, bump-like formations in the surface, mimicking the look of tortoiseshell.

9 Create a template of your glass base by drawing an outline of the plate's inner circle onto tracing paper. If the plate is completely flat, draw a circle that is 1" (25mm) smaller than the edges of the plate. Use this template to cut out a circle from the tortoiseshell clay. Place the clay circle over the center of the plate and press the clay onto the glass with your fingers. Work out any trapped air starting from the center outward. Replace the template over the clay after you've smoothed out any trapped air, and trim away any clay that extends beyond the template edges.

10 Roll out a black clay snake to 24" (61cm) long and approximately ¼" (6mm) in diameter. Run the snake lengthwise through the pasta machine on the largest setting. Trim a straight edge along one side. Press the straight edge of the snake against the tortoiseshell circle, wrapping the entire outer edge. Cut away any excess clay and blend the seam with your fingers.

11 Stipple the black clay border using the stylus to create the appearance of spoon-carved wood. After texturing, trim away the overhanging excess clay, leaving a smooth finish on the plate's edge. Bake the plate at 275° F (135° C) for 30 minutes.

If the clay becomes loose from the glass anytime after baking, carefully slide a clay blade underneath the clay on all sides to remove it from the plate. Reattach the clay to the glass using two-part epoxy.

faux fabergé
enamel pillbox

*C*arl Fabergé was a master artisan known for his glittering, jewel-encrusted eggs and stunning jewelry. Some of Fabergé's most subtle, yet elegant, pieces featured a type of enameling known as guilloche. This amazing technique was often expressed in ripple and ray patterns on clocks and cigarette cases. Many of the pieces that survived Russia's tumultuous history were created in a rose-gold tone. When Fabergé died, the secrets of guilloche enameling died with him. In this project you will create a stylish pillbox that closely mimics this luminous finish.

materials

Polymer clay: gold

Round pillbox: gold

Perfect Pearls mica powder: blush (Ranger Ink)

Gold polymer clay foil

5mm topaz flat-back crystals

Clear UTEE (Ultra Thick Embossing Powder- Ranger)

Crystal rondelle embellishment

Stiff plastic card

1¾" (4cm) circle cutter

Teardrop pattern cutter (Kemper Tools #PC5T)

Plastic spoon

Basic clay kit

1 Cut a 2" x 2" (5cm x 5cm) square of gold polymer clay, rolled out on the largest setting of the pasta machine. Lay the square on a deli sheet. Press lines diagonally through the middle of the square, using a stiff plastic card (like a credit card). Continue to insert lines in the middle of each triangular section until you have marked a total of thirty-two lines, making a ray pattern.

2 Center the circle cutter over the clay square and press. Pull the excess clay away from the cutter, then remove the cutter. Lift the clay circle off the waxed tissue and place it on the lid of the pillbox. Dip the tip of your index finger into the mica powder and brush off any loose powder. Brush your finger lightly over the gold clay circle. Cover the entire raised surface of the clay. This may require dipping your finger in powder several times.

3 Trim and remove a ⅛" (3mm) wide strip of clay from the edge of the gold clay circle, using the craft knife. Roll a 6" (15cm) gold clay snake, ⅛" (3mm) in diameter. Wrap the snake around the outer edge of the gold clay circle, using polymer clay bonder. Blend the seam together with your fingers.

ALTERNATIVE TOOLS

Often in a materials list you'll find a specific product. This doesn't mean you can't complete the project with an alternative tool or material. Visit any craft store or browse through the Internet to find a wealth of alternative tools and products that will give you the similar results. Don't hesitate to use an alternative tool if you have easier access to one, or find a finishing item more to your liking.

4 Roll a large pinch of gold clay through the seventh largest setting of the pasta machine. Burnish a small square of gold polymer clay foil onto the gold clay. See page 18 for information on burnishing.

5 Punch out several gold foil leaves, using the teardrop pattern cutter. Press fine lines into each leaf, using the tip of the needle tool.

7 Use tweezers to place flat-back crystals into the gold clay border between each leaf. Press each crystal into the clay with the tip of your craft knife until the top of the crystal sits level with the clay.

6 Press the foiled leaves around the gold snake border, leaving a space between each leaf.

The plastic insert inside the pillbox must be removed before baking. If the insert doesn't pull out using a gentle tugging, place the entire pillbox in a 275° F (135° C) oven for 10–15 seconds. This should loosen the adhesive and make it easy to pry out the insert while still warm.

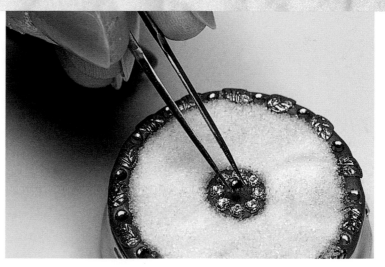

8 Press a small ball of gold clay over the center of the gold clay circle. Spoon small amounts of the embossing powder over the clay circle, taking care not to get any on the clay border or the center clay dot. The embossing powder shouldn't sit higher than the gold clay border. Level the powder with the tip of the craft knife.

9 Press the crystal rondelle over the gold clay center. Bake the pillbox at 275° F (135° C) until the embossing enamel is melted. When the pillbox has cooled, gently pry the clay off the lid using the clay blade. Also remove the rondelle. Reattach these with two-part epoxy.

Gallery Idea

To create interesting variations on this project, impress the center clay with a texture plate or rubber stamp instead of creating the ray pattern. Apply mica powder to the raised surface as in step 2, and complete the project as instructed.

gifts to wear

*A*ccessorizing ourselves with jewelry and other adornments is a uniquely human trait found in every culture throughout history. Personal adornment is the oldest form of self-expression. Jewelry and wearable accessories are a great way of enhancing our clothing, expressing our mood or revealing our personality. Learn how to make wonderful wearables that are suitable for every day or a special occasion. Working with the transfer, millefiori, faux finishing and stamping techniques used in these projects will enable you to create fun, funky, functional and heirloom-quality adornments.

projects

floral millefiori
watch face

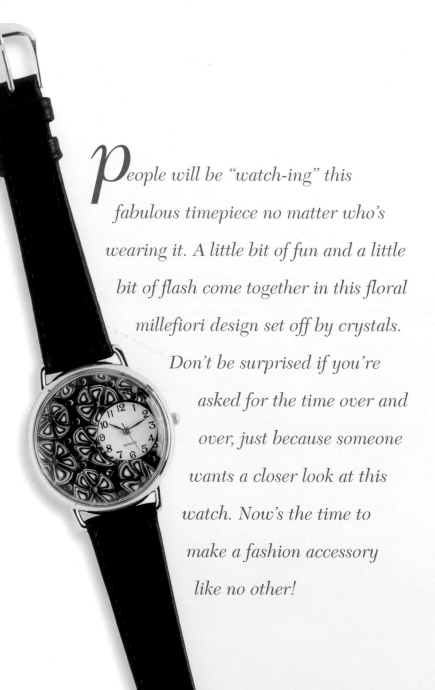

*P*eople will be "watch-ing" this fabulous timepiece no matter who's wearing it. A little bit of fun and a little bit of flash come together in this floral millefiori design set off by crystals. Don't be surprised if you're asked for the time over and over, just because someone wants a closer look at this watch. Now's the time to make a fashion accessory like no other!

materials

Polymer clay: black, violet, blue and 2 blocks of white

Paintable watch face (National Artcraft)

Twelve 5mm flat-back crystals

Large knitting needle

1¼" (3cm) circle template

⅝" (16mm) circle pattern cutter (Kemper Tools #PCAR)

Black fine-tip permanent marker

Paintbrush

Basic clay kit

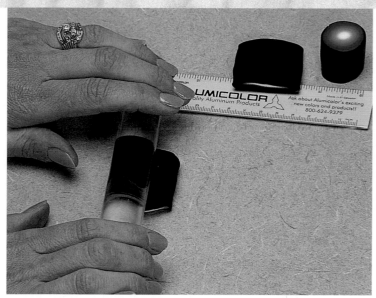

1 Make three Skinner blend canes: black/white, violet/white and blue/white. Wrap the violet and blue canes with a layer of black clay rolled out through the fifth largest setting of the pasta machine. Cut 2" (5cm) sections of each wrapped cane. Hand-compress the black/white cane to flatten it to 1½" (4cm) wide. Repeat this step with the violet/white cane. Roll and reduce the blue and white cane to ½" (13mm) in diameter. Trim the reduced cane to ½" (13mm).

2 Stack the violet/white cane over the black/white cane. Roll the knitting needle down the center (lengthwise) of the violet/white cane to make a troughlike depression. Set the blue/white cane lengthwise into this trough. Pull the edges of the stacked, flattened canes up and around the blue/white cane. Pinch the cane into a teardrop shape.

3 Roll and reduce this cane to 7" (18cm) long (see the sidebar on page 46). Pinch the cane into a teardrop shape between your thumb and forefinger along the side where the black/white and the violet/white canes meet.

4 Trim the distorted ends from the reduced cane and cut it into six 1" (25mm) sections. Assemble the six sections in a circular formation, with the pointed end in, to create a six-petal flower cane.

5 Compress the cane to remove any air pockets. Cut off a 1" (25mm) section and reduce it ³/₈" (10mm) in diameter. Save the remaining cane for more watches or another project. Cut twelve to fourteen thin slices from the cane with the clay blade and place them randomly over a 1½" x 1½" (4cm x 4cm) sheet of black clay rolled through the fourth largest setting of the pasta machine.

TEARDROP CANE REDUCTION

For teardrop-shaped canes, pinch the cane along one length, following the pattern such as the center vein of a leaf cane. Reducing a cane by rolling can twist the design. To make sure the cane is properly aligned while shaping, pinch both ends of the cane in the desired shape. If the pinched ends don't line-up parallel to one another, twist the ends to realign them. Once the pattern runs straight, continue to pinch through the center along the entire length of the cane to reduce it.

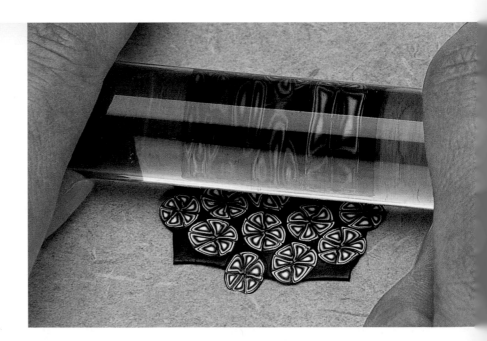

6 Roll the acrylic rod over the surface until the cane slices have melded seamlessly onto the black clay sheet. Run the flowered sheet through the fifth and sixth largest settings of the pasta machine.

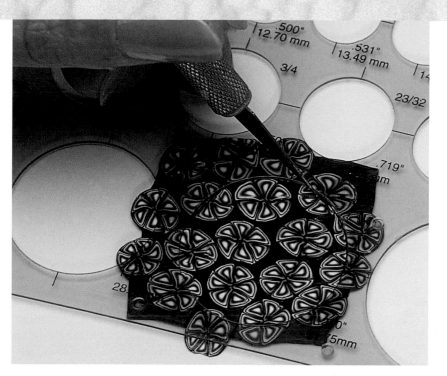

7 Place the embedded sheet on a ceramic work tile. Position the 1¼" (3cm) circle template over the patterned clay. Cut around the inside edge of the circle with the craft knife. The blade of the knife should be pointed and very sharp. Lift the template away and remove the excess clay.

8 Press the circle pattern cutter into the clay circle ¹⁄₁₆" (2mm) away from the edge. Leave the cutter in place. Put a crystal over the center of every flower. Press the crystals into the clay using the tip of the craft knife. Lift away the pattern cutter. If the cut circle doesn't come up with the cutter, leave it in place during baking. Bake on the tile at 275° F (135° C) for 30 minutes. When the clay is cool, slide the clay blade underneath to remove it from the tile. Remove the clay circle if left in place during baking.

Embellish the watchband by painting it with acrylic paint or adding flat-back crystals or charms with epoxy.

tip

9 Draw a black line around the inside edge of the clock frame with the black marker. This line should be about ¹⁄₈" (3mm) thick. Brush a small amount of polymer clay bonder on the back of the clay face. Position the open circle over the clock face and press the clay disk in place. After the glue has had a few seconds to set, brush polymer clay bonder on a few spots along the bottom edge of the watch crystal and press the crystal into place.

heirloom photo
bracelet

*P*ermanently preserve pictures of loved ones, past or present, using a unique transfer method discovered by Beckah Krahula. No need to sacrifice the original picture to make these mini photo tiles. You'll only need a color photocopy. The photo tiles are interchangeable so they can be swapped on the wearer's whim. Wear photos of your ancestors one day, your kids or pets the next. Stamped clay beads set off each frame for a stylish look.

materials

Polymer clay: black and pearl (or white)	Inexpensive gin	Wire cutters
Liquid polymer clay	Acrylic floor wax or water-based sealer	Oval pattern cutter (Kemper Tools #PCBO)
Rectangular photo charm bracelet, gold or silver (Memory Maker Bracelet)	Two 10" (25cm) pieces of 1mm stretch jewelry cord (clear)	Paintbrush
Five or six 1" x ¾" (25mm x 19mm) color toner-based photocopies (no inkjet or laser prints)	Small metallic spacer beads, gold or silver	Needle-nose pliers
10" (25cm) of 20-gauge wire	Large rose star stamp (Stamp Oasis #776H)	Basic clay kit
	Silver pigment stamp pad (Ranger)	

1 Use wire cutters to cut the wire into ten 1" (25mm) sections.

2 To make the connector beads, roll out black clay on the second largest setting of the pasta machine. Punch out ten ovals with the pattern cutter. Press a wire section horizontally into the top and bottom sections of five ovals, dividing each into thirds. One half of the wire should be embedded into the clay. Make sure that the wires are placed in the same positions on each oval.

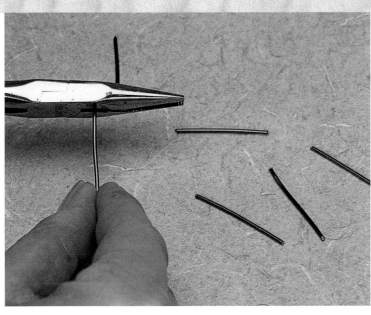

BEAD VARIATIONS

Try making the connector beads using circle, star or heart-shaped cutters. Instead of stamping, try adding shaped cutouts or millefiori cane slices onto the bead faces for a different look.

3 Place the other five ovals directly over the wire-embedded ovals. Carefully lift each oval from your work surface and blend the side seams together. Round the top edges of the layered ovals with your fingertip. Ink the stamp and press the stamp onto each oval. Reink the stamp for each oval. Bake the pieces at 275º F (135º C) for 30 minutes.

4 Use the photo reduction template that comes with each bracelet to size your photocopies. Cut out each photo. Leave a ¼" (6mm) border around the area that will be framed in the bracelet. Place a photo facedown over pearl clay that has been rolled through the fourth largest setting of the pasta machine. Burnish the photo onto the clay by rubbing it with your index finger for several seconds. Dip your finger into the gin and saturate the photocopy. Let the photo sit for a few minutes, then resaturate it with gin. Start rolling your index finger back and forth over the center of the paper until the paper starts to come off in small rolls. When the paper starts to dry, resaturate the image with a very small amount of gin. Repeat until all the paper is removed.

5 Cut and discard the elastic bands holding the bracelet together. Remove the acetate rectangles from each of the picture frames with the tip of a craft knife. Save one to use as a cutting template. Position the acetate template over the transfers and cut away the excess clay with the craft knife.

IMAGE TRANSFER

You may try other types of alcohol for image transfer, but inexpensive gin seems to work the best. This process isn't difficult, but requires patience. Use a light touch. Do not apply too much pressure or you may remove the toner-based image. Let the clay dry between alcohol applications. Any remaining paper fiber will appear when dry, giving the image a frosted appearance. It may take as many as 8–12 alcohol applications before the clay surface is completely free of paper fiber. If you find you are removing the image, you are rubbing too hard or applying too much pressure. Use a magnifying glass to help determine if all the paper is gone. When all the paper is removed, the clay surface should feel like plain, uncured clay (slightly tacky).

6 Brush a thin layer of liquid polymer clay over each transfer. Bake the transfers at 275° F (135° C) for 30 minutes.

8 Remove the wires from each of the baked oval beads with the pliers. Apply a thin coat of acrylic floor wax or water-based sealer over each bead to protect the stamped design. Allow the beads to dry.

7 When cool, bend the baked transfers slightly and insert them under the frame's corners.

10 To hide the knots, finish stringing at the center of one frame. Tie the cord ends together, knotting 2–3 times. Trim excess cord and reverse the bracelet.

9 Attach a piece of tape to one end of each stringing cord. Working with the pieces facedown, thread a picture frame onto the stretch cords, then thread spacer beads, followed by a connector bead. Continue stringing the beads and frames using this pattern until the bracelet is the desired length. Remove the tape and add a spacer bead.

For a larger bracelet, use all six frames. For a small wrist, set one frame aside. For a child's bracelet, string only four frames. These extra picture frames can be used to make a matching pin, or pendant, or as a crafting embellishment for scrapbooks and such.

tip

faux mother-of-pearl
plumeria pendant

*M*other-of-pearl is one of nature's most beautiful materials. Learn to re-create the look of this gem of the seas using polymer clay. This project features a new and exciting way to seal the surface treatment and create the glasslike appearance of polished mother-of-pearl, all without laborious sanding and polishing! You'll learn how to make a "slide-lock" clasp, so your creation can be worn with a variety of necklines, including choker, midlength for V-necks and scoop necks, and amulet length, depending on your fashion mood. Make a matching set of earrings to complete the look.

materials

- Polymer clay: pearl or white
- Liquid polymer clay
- Pearlescent polymer clay foil
- 30" (76cm) rubber (buna) cord
- Three sterling silver jump rings

- Two sterling silver French earring wires
- Teardrop pattern cutters
  (Kemper Tools large #PCBT, small #PCJT)
- Ballpoint pen
- Poster tack

- Craft stick
- Two pairs of needle-nose or jewelry pliers
- Knitting needle
- Paintbrush
- Basic clay kit

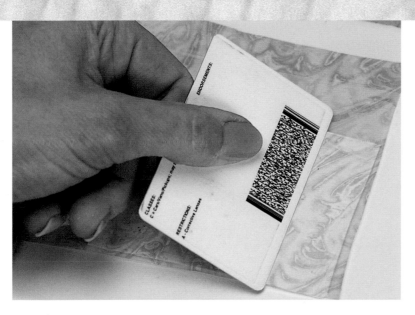

FOILING

You can help the foiling process by flash-heating the clay with a heat gun. Hold the gun at least 6"–8" (15cm–20cm) away from the clay. Move it back and forth over the foil-covered clay to heat the foil. Heat the foil for no more than 5–7 seconds. Immediately reburnish the foil and tear away the backing quickly. Do not overheat the clay or hold the gun too close. This will begin the curing process, making the clay unusable.

1 Roll out ⅛ block of either pearl or white clay on the fourth largest setting of the pasta machine. Burnish a sheet of pearlescent polymer clay foil over the clay. See pages 15 and 18 for foil application tips.

2 Cut out five teardrop pieces using the larger pattern cutter. The teardrops should be about ½" x ¾" (13mm x 19mm). Smooth the edges of each petal with your fingers for a finished look. Impress three to five fine, wavy lines in the surface of each petal with the needle tool. Start these lines at the pointed end, drawing them ½ to ¾ of the length down each petal.

3 Slightly pinch the rounded end of each petal between your thumb and forefinger to form a raised tip.

4 Place the lower half (pointed tip inward) of the first petal over a second petal (scallop fashion). Repeat this step with the three remaining petals. Finish by placing the last petal so that it slightly tucks under the first petal, creating a pinwheel effect. Adjust the petals as necessary to make sure they are evenly spaced. Make a small hole close to the end of one petal with the needle tool. This hole should be large enough for the jump ring to hang freely when threaded on the rubber cord.

To make the pendant easier to handle while applying the epoxy, attach the flower to a craft stick with a large ball of poster tack.

tip

5 Roll a small ball of pearl clay, cut from the excess foiled clay, and place it in the center of the flower. Press the tip of a retracted ballpoint pen into the middle of this ball. Bake the flower at 275º F (135º C) for 30 minutes and allow the clay to cool completely.

6   Mix quarter-size puddles of two-part epoxy. Use a toothpick to apply a thick layer of epoxy over the entire pendant. This seals the foil and creates the glasslike look of polished mother-of-pearl. Epoxy has a tendency to puddle toward the middle of the pendant until it thickens. While the glue is still uncured, continue to spread it toward the edges with a toothpick. Stop spreading the epoxy once you notice strings forming when you lift away the toothpick—usually a few minutes after mixing.

7   Cut two large teardrops of clay from the leftover foiled clay sheet. Roll each piece into a ball. Form each ball into a teardrop by rolling one side with the tip of your finger. Make sure the larger end of the teardrop is large enough to fit on the end of the cord.

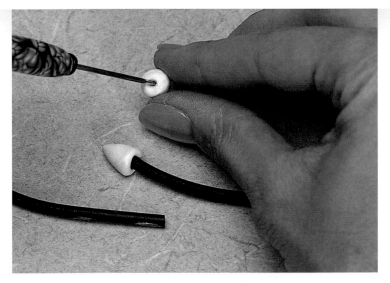

A second coat of epoxy may need to be applied if the first coat has shrunk away from the edge of the pendant while drying.

tip

8   Insert a needle tool halfway into the rounded end of the teardrop. Rotate the needle tool slightly to enlarge the hole. Press the end of the rubber cord into the hole and remove. Repeat this step with the second ball.

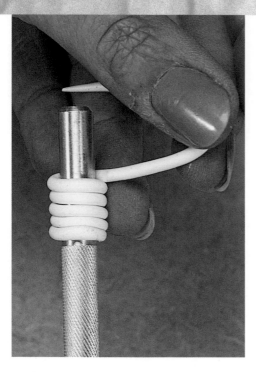

9 Roll a 5" (13cm) long by ⅛" (3mm) diameter rope of white clay. Roll the ends into a point with your fingertips. Wrap the clay tightly around the handle of a needle tool or knitting needle to form a coil.

10 Brush the coil of clay with a thin layer of liquid polymer clay. Suspend the knitting needle on the edges of a small, clay-dedicated baking pan. Bake the coil and teardrop cord ends at 275° F (135° C) for 30 minutes.

To determine the correct size knitting needle or handle for the rubber cord you've chosen, fold the cord so that two strands sit side by side. The needle should be the same thickness or slightly larger than the combined cords. If the needle is smaller than the combined diameters of the cord, the coil will be too tight. If the needle is much larger than the combined diameter, the coil will be too loose and won't provide enough friction to hold the cords at the desired length.

tip

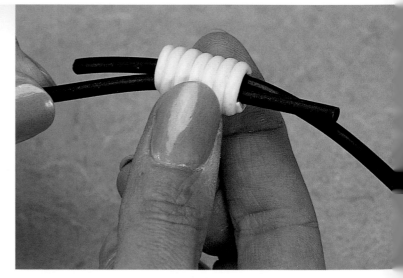

To prevent the coil from cracking as it cools, twist and slide it off the needle while it is still warm to the touch.

tip

11 Slip a third of the cord through the cooled coil. Insert the other end of the cord through the opposite end of the coil. There will be resistance when you attempt to do this since the coil will be snug with two cords inside of it. Press the second cord end in as far as possible, using the needle tool if necessary. Once the cord is in as far as it can be pushed, slowly pull the opposite end of the cord that was inserted first. This should pull the second cord end out the other side.

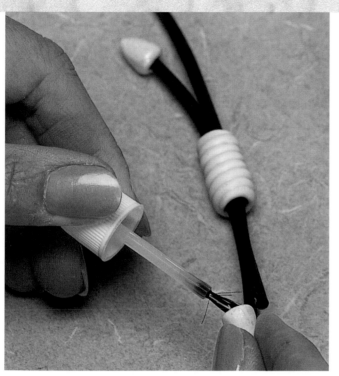

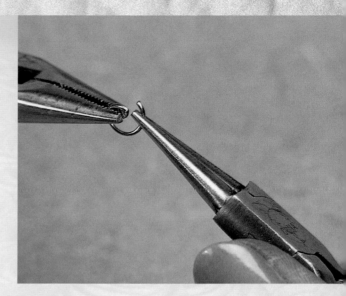

12 Glue the cooled, clay teardrops onto the cord ends with polymer clay bonder. These teardrops prevent the cords from ever being pulled all the way out. After the epoxied flower has cured for 24 hours, attach it to the cord with a silver jump ring.

JUMP RINGS

When opening a jump ring, twist one end toward you with one pair of pliers while twisting the other end away from you with another pair of pliers. Pulling the ring open with the ends directly opposite one another will distort the shape. Close the ring by twisting the ends back together until they are aligned.

Gallery Idea

To make earrings, follow steps 1–6 of the instructions, using the small teardrop pattern cutter. Attach the cured flowers to the earring wires with a jump ring.

Asian minaudière
purse

*M*inaudière is the French
word for a tiny handbag or purse.
Whether the wearer is spending
an evening out dancing or
dining, this purse is sure to
take center stage. Faux
cinnabar and genuine
pearls perfectly accent
this highly detailed
work of art. You'll also
learn how to antique
embossed polymer
clay while making
this elaborately
elegant club bag.

materials

Polymer clay: black, red, brown and white

Small metal purse (Heart in Hand Studio)

Petroleum jelly

Iridescent pearl acrylic paint

Acrylic floor wax

Assorted white fresh-water pearls

Asian newsprint stamp (Hero Arts #S1610)

Floral pattern stamp
(Magenta Rubber Stamps #14437P)

Silver pigment ink stamp pad (Ranger)

Flower stamp (Leather Factory #W532)

Needle-nose pliers

Protective eyewear

Rotary tool with carbide bit (Dremel #192)

Scissors

Thin knitting needle

Pillow batting

Automotive-grade wet/dry
600-grit sandpaper

Basic clay kit

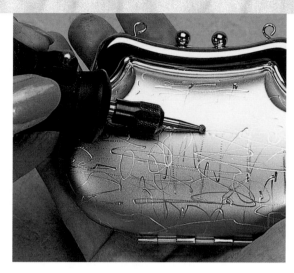

1 Use the pliers to open the eye pin connecting the shoulder chain to the purse. Remove the chain and set it aside. Wear protective eyewear while using a rotary tool to rough up both sides of the purse. This will allow the epoxy to adhere to the purse. Note: The purse is completed one side at a time. This prevents accidental marring of the clay due to the extensive amount of handling that is required for this project.

2 Roll out one block of black clay on the third largest setting of the pasta machine. Imprint the clay with the Asian newsprint stamp. Press firmly enough to leave a deep impression. Mix dime-size portions of two-part epoxy on an index card. Spread a thin, even layer of epoxy over the surface of the purse. Do not apply glue to the upper edges. Carefully place the stamped clay onto the face of the purse. Gently press from the center, working out any trapped air toward the clay edges. Be sure that the stamped clay lettering is sitting straight before the glue sets. Allow the epoxy to set for 5 minutes before starting step 3.

Apply petroleum jelly to the hinge before applying epoxy. This will keep the glue from fusing the hinge together.

tip

3 Trim the excess clay from the sides and along the top edge of the purse face with the craft knife. Be sure the clay edges are pressed firmly against the purse sides. Bake the purse at 275° F (135° C) for 25 minutes.

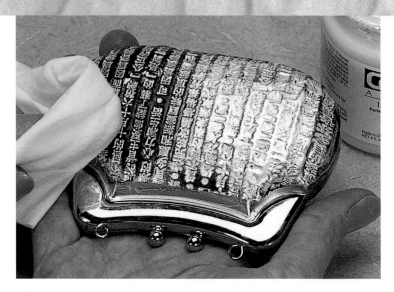

4 When the clay has cooled, rub pearl acrylic paint into the stamped impressions with your index finger. Wipe the excess paint away with a damp paper towel. Be careful not to wipe paint out of the stamped letters. Let the paint dry for about 20–30 minutes. Sand the clay with wet/dry sandpaper. Do not immerse the purse in water. Frequently rinse the sandpaper to remove accumulated grit. Sanding is complete when all the paint on the top surface of the clay is removed and the surface is satiny smooth. Polish the clay and finish with a layer of acrylic floor wax. See page 15 for instructions on polishing.

5 While the acrylic sealer is drying, make cinnabar clay. Mix ½ block of red clay with ⅛ block of brown clay. Mix the clay by hand or through the pasta machine until thoroughly blended. Roll the cinnabar through the third largest setting of the pasta machine. Ink the floral stamp with the silver pad.

6 Spray automotive protectant spray on one side of the cinnabar clay sheet and spread it over the surface with your fingers. Carefully place the clay with the sprayed side up on top of the floral stamp. Roll the acrylic rod over the clay in a single, firm pass. Remove the clay from the stamp and lay the clay faceup.

7 Trace the fan shape onto a deli sheet and cut it out. Lay the fan template over the stamped cinnabar clay. Trim around the template and remove excess clay. Make two fans, setting one aside for the other half of the purse. Attach one fan to the center of the black clay with a small amount of epoxy. Allow the glue to set for 5 minutes.

8 Impress diagonal lines in the fan with the knitting needle, inking the needle each time with the silver stamp pad. The lines should be spaced so that they are very close together at the bottom and ¼" (6mm) apart at the top of the fan.

9 Roll an 8" (20cm) long and ⅛" (3mm) diameter snake of black clay. Glue the snake around the outer edge of the fan with polymer clay bonder. Trim any excess clay and blend the seams together with your finger.

Use this fan pattern for the Asian Minaudière Purse. Enlarge or reduce as necessary.

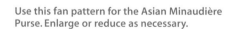
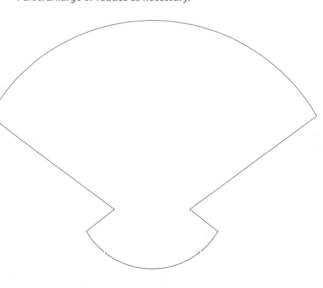

10 Make a cinnabar and white Skinner blend cane. Roll and reduce this cane to ³⁄₈" (10mm) in diameter. Cut off a ¹⁄₂" (13mm) section and set it aside. Pinch the rest of the cane between your thumb and index finger along the entire length to form a teardrop shape. Cut several dozen slices to ¹⁄₁₆" (2mm) thick with a clay blade. Starting on one side of the purse, glue cane slices in a scalloped fashion, tip over end, along the clay-covered edges. The outer edge of each slice should be lined up flush with the edges of the purse. Stop placing slices when you reach the middle of the purse at the bottom. Repeat this process on the opposite side of the purse until the slices meet. Make sure you don't cover the hinges. Cut a thin slice from the ¹⁄₂" (13mm) round cane you set aside earlier. Glue this slice over the bottom center where the cane slices meet. Press a pearl into this slice. With the purse open, trim any overhanging clay away from the edges, using the craft knife. Bake at 275° F (135° C) for 30 minutes.

11 Roll out a 12" (30cm) long by ¹⁄₈" (3mm) diameter cinnabar snake. Cut it in half and place the pieces side by side. Glue the doubled snake between the top metal border and the black clay face. Trim excess clay away from the purse sides with the craft knife.

The pearls can easily fall off after baking if not permanently attached. Once the purse has cooled, pry off the pearls using the tip of the craft knife. Reattach them with two-part epoxy to secure them permanently.

tip

12 Roll a 1" (25mm) long, ¹⁄₁₆" (2mm) diameter cinnabar snake. Cut this snake into three ³⁄₈" (10mm) long sections. Place the sections side by side. Use polymer clay bonder to glue them vertically over the middle of the double cinnabar snake, just below the purse clasp. Press a pearl into the middle of this triple snake embellishment.

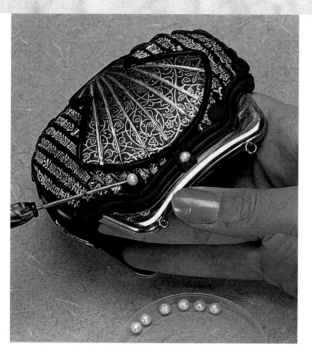

13 Roll four ¼" (6mm) diameter balls of cinnabar clay. Glue them beneath the double cinnabar border at the outside corners and the points where the curve bends upward. Press a pearl into each of these balls.

14 Roll out the remaining cinnabar clay on the fourth largest setting of the pasta machine. Emboss the clay four times with the leather flower stamp. Cut out the clay flowers with the craft knife. Glue the flowers on the black clay around the clay shell. Press a small pearl into the center of each flower. Place the purse on a small square of pillow batting. Bake the purse with the batting on a tile at 275° F (135° C) for 30 minutes. When the purse is cool, repeat steps 2–14 on the unfinished side. When finished, reattach the shoulder chain to the purse using the needle-nose pliers.

Gallery Ideas

Dress up the shoulder chain with pearls and beads. Cut the chain to 26" (66cm) long with wire cutters. Attach two 6½" (17cm) long beaded strands at both ends. For this purse, rose tulip beads were strung on a 10" (25cm) long piece of tiger tail wire. Start by making a small loop at one end and securing it with a crimp bead. String the beads and pearls in the following order: tulip bead (with the wide end facing the end loop), black pearl, tulip bead (facing the opposite direction of the first bead), white pearl. Repeat this sequence six more times. Finish the strand with a loop secured with another crimp bead. Cut the excess wire with cutters. Repeat on a second 10" (25cm) piece of tiger tail wire. Attach the strands to the shoulder chain using silver-colored split rings. Attach the beaded shoulder chain to the loops on the purse.

teardrop
wire choker

*t*his elegant neck-

lace will complement any neckline.

Millefiori cane slices become simple

teardrop beads that gracefully dangle

from a scalloped chain. Coiled wire and

miracle bead accents complete the look of

this distinctive and fashionable choker

that's certain to never go out of style.

This creation works as well with a

sweater and blue jeans as it does

with a little black dress.

materials

Polymer clay: 1 block of violet, black, white and green

Gold-filled 16" (41cm) scallop choker (Rio Grande)

Green-coated 22-gauge craft wire (Toner)

Eleven 2" (5cm) gold-filled eye pins

Twelve 3mm glass miracle beads: colors such as violet, fuchsia, green

Round-nose pliers

Needle-nose pliers with wire cutter

Round tapered and flat metal files

Basic clay kit

1 Make two Skinner blend canes: violet/white and green/white. Cut 1" (25mm) sections of each. Stand the violet Skinner blend cane on its end and cut down through the middle with the clay blade. Insert a black clay vein along one cane half. Reassemble and wrap, following the instructions in step 8, on page 32. Reduce the cane to 3½" (9cm) in length. Cut off the distorted ends. Cut the cane into three 1" (25mm) sections. Combine these sections together like a clover leaf, with the intersecting black lines pointing out from the center.

2 Roll and reduce the green/white Skinner blend cane to 3½" (9cm) long. Pinch the cane along its length between your thumb and index finger to create a triangular shape. Cut off the distorted ends and divide the cane into three 1" (25mm) sections. Place each of the green sections, pointed side inward, into the violet cane formation. Compress the cane and wrap it with a sheet of black clay rolled through the sixth largest setting of the pasta machine.

If the cane is very soft after forming and the shape becomes distorted after cutting, gently reshape the slice with your fingers.

tip

3 Roll and reduce the cane until it is ¾" (19mm) in diameter. Cut a ½" (13mm) section from this cane and pinch it between your thumb and index finger to form a teardrop. Trim away one distorted end. Cut a 1/16" (2mm) slice from the cane. Put a hole near the top of the slice with the needle tool. For this and the following steps, always pinch the canes so that one of the violet sections is pointing straight up.

4 Cut a ½" (13mm) section from the remaining cane. Roll and reduce it to ½" (13mm) in diameter. Trim away one distorted end and cut four ¹⁄₁₆" (2mm) thick slices from the cane. Cut a ½" (13mm) section from the remaining cane section. Reduce to ⅜" (10mm) in diameter. Cut four ¹⁄₁₆" (2mm) thick slices from this cane. Place holes near the top of all these slices with the needle tool. Bake the nine slices on the unwaxed side of a deli sheet. Bake at 275° F (135° C) for 25 minutes.

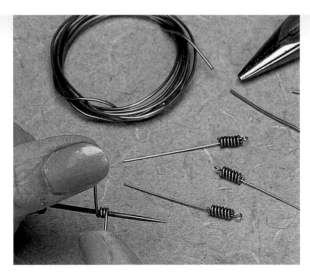

5 Cut nine 2" (5cm) sections of green-coated wire. Form nine coils by wrapping each piece of wire around the tip of the needle tool.

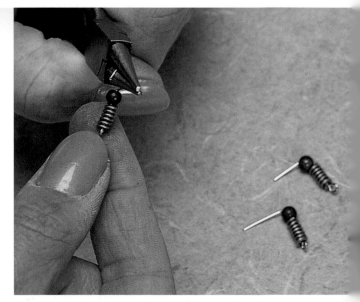

6 Place a coiled wire over an eye pin and add a miracle bead. Bend the remaining length of the eye pin at a 90° angle. Cut the bent wire to ⅜" (10mm) long. Grasp the wire end with round-nose pliers. Bend the wire over toward the coil to form a loop. A bead may be added to both sides of the wire coil. Mix and match the bead colors or use just one or two as desired.

tip

Smooth the ends of the green coil wire with a metal file.

tip
See page 57 for tips on opening and closing jump rings and eye pins.

7 Open the loops you just made in the previous step. Enlarge the hole in the cane slices, using a round tapered file, so that the components swing freely from the eye pins. Thread the cooled cane slices onto the loops, and close the loops to secure.

8 Attach the wire and clay components to the choker chain. Open the eyes of each component and attach them to the links connecting the gold scallops of the chain. Start with the largest component in the middle. Add two medium slices on either side of the large one. Finish by adding two small slices on either side of the medium slices for a graduated look.

CUTTING CANES

Slicing a cane immediately after reduction can result in distorted slices. Kato Polyclay can usually be cut a few minutes after reduction with minimal or no distortion. For Premo Sculpey and Fimo clays, allow the canes to rest one to two days before slicing, or freeze them for 15–20 minutes to firm the clay. Canes thaw very quickly, so repeated freezing may be necessary. A clean, sharp blade is essential to successful cane slicing. Even new blades pick up clay residue from repeated slicing, causing the blade to drag. This drag factor can make cutting thin, even slices more difficult and can result in smeared patterns. Clean your blade frequently, using the cleaning and sharpening tips on page 13.

For round canes, use a back and forth sawing motion. For teardrop canes, use a single, sweeping cut from the widest end of the cane, down toward the tip. Flip the cane over after every slice to help maintain the cane's shape. For triangular or square canes, gently saw the blade into the cane just enough to embed it, then slice directly down. Follow by rotating the canes one turn before each slice.

home décor *gifts*

*W*hat graces a room more than beautiful artwork? What about artwork that has not only beauty and form, but function as well? This section features décor gifts ideal for a variety of interiors from contemporary to earthy; and romantic to Asian motifs. You'll learn how to create gifts that help you get organized, cast a warm glow, show off your prized photos, hold a fragrant potpourri and help keep track of the time. You'll enjoy creating décor gifts using innovative layering, Incaré, inlay, transfer and punch construction techniques.

projects

tumbling leaves
key rack

*W*ant to end the scramble to locate those misplaced keys? With this project you'll learn how to create a lovely and functional rack perfect for organizing your keys. Inlaid leaves gracefully tumble across a crackled, gold surface. This elegant rack is also ideal for holding other items such as jewelry and small accessories with style.

materials

Polymer clay:
black and 2 blocks of pearl

Liquid polymer clay

Four-hook organizer rack

Iridescent gold acrylic paint

Paintbrushes

Screwdriver

Leaf-shaped paper punches

Pattern cutters: large heart, medium heart
and a small circle (Kemper Tools #PCAH,
#PC1H and #PC4C)

Clay gun with small
three-leaf clover die

Basic clay kit

1 Roll out a 2½" x 5" (6cm x 13cm) sheet of pearl clay on the largest
setting of the pasta machine. Brush a thick coat of gold acrylic paint
over the pearl clay and set it aside to dry. Loosen the four screws in the
back of the key rack and remove the hooks.

2 Roll out a 5" x 5" (13cm x 13cm) sheet of black clay on the seventh
largest setting of the pasta machine. Place the clay sheet on the
waxed side of a deli sheet and roll it again through the seventh largest
setting of the pasta machine. Place the clay on the deli sheet, facedown
on a clean ceramic tile. Make sure there are no air bubbles in the clay.
Bake it at 275º F (135º C) for 15 minutes. When the clay is cool, peel off
the deli sheet, then cut out several leaves from the baked clay sheet, using
the leaf punches.

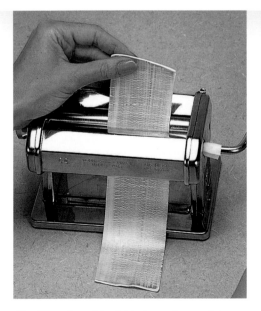

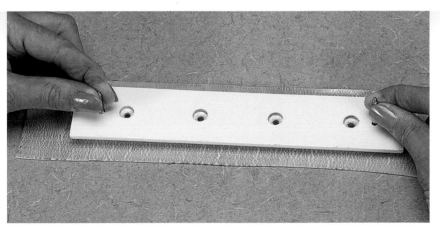

3 When the gold paint is dry on the pearl clay,
roll the clay lengthwise through the second
largest setting of the pasta machine. Continue rolling
the sheet through in the same direction, reducing the
width of the rollers until you reach the fifth largest
setting of the machine. This will crackle the dried paint.

4 Insert the backing screws through the back of the key rack. Turn the rack over and press
it in place over the center of the crackled pearl clay. Push the screws down lightly and
remove them along with the rack. Cut out the circle indentations made by the screws with a
circle pattern cutter. Remove these circles with the tip of a craft knife.

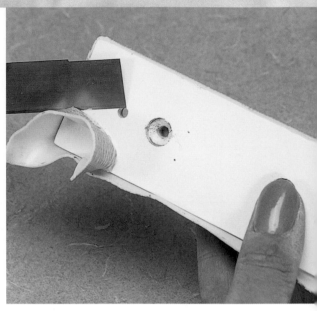

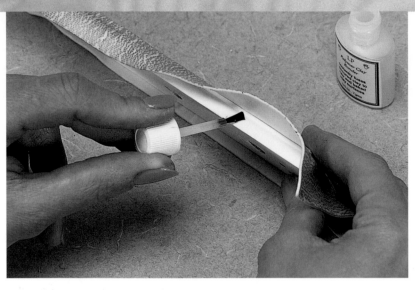

5 Brush a thin layer of liquid polymer clay over the raised section of the key rack. Place the painted pearl clay sheet over the rack, aligning the holes with the screws. Press out any air bubbles with your fingers. Glue down the sides with polymer clay bonder.

6 Cut off the excess clay from the bottom and sides of the rack with a clay blade. Save the trimmed pearl clay for later.

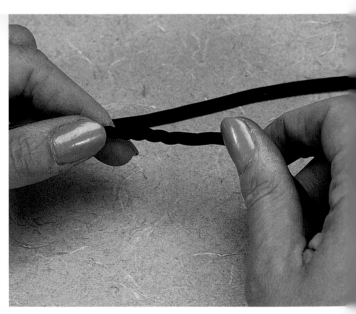

7 Cut the excess clay away from the screw and hook holes with the craft knife.

tip If you have trouble extruding the clay, mix in a little liquid clay before you load the gun. Turn to page 19 for more ideas on using the clay gun.

8 Load the clay gun with black clay and the small clover die. Extrude 24" (61cm) of the clay. Twist the snake into a rope and glue it around the raised portion of the key rack with polymer clay bonder. Trim away the excess clay.

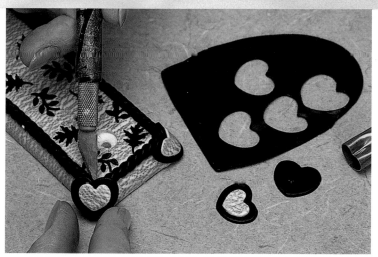

9 Holding a single black clay leaf with tweezers, brush a small amount of polymer clay bonder on the back of the leaf. Press leaves randomly on the crackled gold surface of the rack. Cut some of the punched leaves in half, using straight and diagonal cuts, for placement along the rope border. Use the tip of the craft knife to embed the leaves into the clay.

10 Using the large heart cutter, cut out four black clay hearts from a sheet rolled through the fourth largest setting of the pasta machine. Cut out four hearts from the leftover painted pearl clay, using the medium heart cutter. Place a smaller heart over the center of each black heart. Glue these hearts at each corner. Use your fingers to gently bend the hearts to fit the contours of the key rack.

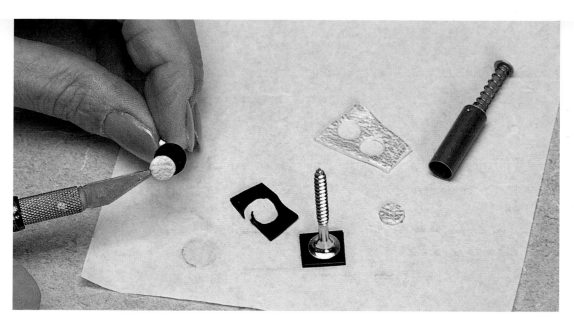

11 Cut two small squares from the black clay rolled out on the fifth largest setting of the pasta machine. Place the clay onto a deli sheet, and press the attachment screws facedown on the black clay. Cut around the screw head with the clay blade and lift the screw, with the black clay in place, away from the deli sheet. Punch out two pearl circles from the leftover painted clay, using the circle cutter. Roll these circles into balls and press them onto the black clay, covering the screw heads. Loosely screw the hooks back into place. Bake the rack and the clay-covered screws at 275° F (135° C) for 30 minutes. When the rack is cool, tighten the hook screws into place. Pry off the clay covers from the screw heads. Hang the rack to the wall. If you like, cover the screw heads by attaching clay covers with poster tack.

Incaré polymer
clay clock

*t*here's always time for clay. At least clay is what everyone

will think about when they consult this unique timepiece. The

paper lacing technique known as Incaré is adapted to clay to

create a delicate, dimensional effect. You'll also learn how to

texture clay to get the look of spoon-carved wood. After seeing

this unusual clock, you'll be looking for the time to make one

for all your friends and family!

materials

Polymer clay: red, gold, pearl
and 2 blocks of black

Liquid polymer clay

7" (18cm) round wood clock base
(Walnut Hollow)

¾" (19mm) stem clock
components (Walnut Hollow)

Picture frame hanger

Tracing paper

Paintbrush

Large ball-tip stylus

Small piece of hook and loop
fastener (with stiff hooks)

Paper lacing template (Lacé #8)

Circle pattern cutter
(Kemper Tools #PC5R)

Teardrop pattern cutters
(Kemper Tools large #PCBT
and medium #PCC3)

Basic clay kit

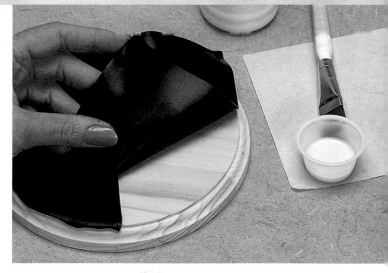

1 Trace the numbers 1–12 onto a 4" x 5" (10cm x 13cm) piece of tracing paper. Each number should be ¾"–1" tall (19mm–25mm). Roll out a 4" x 5" (10cm x 13cm) sheet of pearl clay on the fourth largest setting of the pasta machine. Place the clay sheet on a ceramic work tile. Lay the tracing paper template over the clay and burnish with your fingertips. Cut out the numbers with the craft knife (a new, pointed blade should be used). Remove the tracing paper and cut through the numbers one more time to make sure they are cleanly cut. Lift away the excess clay. Leave the numbers on the tile and bake at 275° F (135° C) for 20 minutes.

Choose the font or style of number you want for your clock and print it from a computer. For this clock, I used a font called Magneto at 56-point size.

tip

2 Brush a thin layer of liquid polymer clay over the raised surface of the wood clock base. Roll out two 6½" x 3½" (17cm x 9cm) sheets of black clay on the third largest setting of the pasta machine. Cut and assemble these sheets onto the clock base. Trim the excess clay from the raised edge of the clock base. Poke the needle tool through the back of the clock base to mark the center hole. Use this mark as a gauge for cutting the clay away from the center opening with the craft knife.

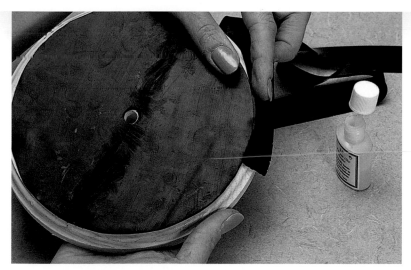

3 Roll a 1" x 24" (3cm x 61cm) strip of black clay through the third largest setting of the pasta machine. Cut a straight edge along one side of the strip. Glue this clay to the edge of the clock base with polymer clay bonder. The glue dries quickly, especially on wood. Apply the glue and clay in small increments until the entire outer edge is covered. Cut off the excess clay and blend the seam with your fingers. Cut excess clay away from the bottom edge of the clock base with the clay blade. Stipple the black clay border using the large ball-tip stylus.

4 Blend a large pinch of black clay into a block of red clay to create burgundy clay. Roll a 5" x 5" (13cm x 13cm) sheet of burgundy clay using the sixth largest setting of the pasta machine and place it on a deli sheet. Roll a 5" x 5" (13cm x 13cm) sheet of gold clay through the fourth largest setting of the pasta machine. Lay the gold clay sheet over the burgundy clay. Be careful to not trap air between these sheets.

5 Remove the deli sheet from the burgundy and gold clay square. Place the clay square with the burgundy faceup over a fresh sheet of deli paper. Repeatedly press the stiff side of a hook and loop fastener into the burgundy clay to texture the surface.

6 Place a deli sheet over the textured burgundy clay. Lay the paper lacing template over the burgundy clay and cut through the V-shaped marks with the craft knife. Cut around the edge of the template with the craft knife and remove the excess clay, leaving a circle. Mark through the center hole of the template with the needle tool. Remove the template and the top layer deli sheet from the clay.

LAYERING CLAY

To avoid introducing air between layers of clay, press the two sheets together along one edge. Pull the remaining top sheet up and over an acrylic rod. Slowly roll the rod across the length of the two sheets with one hand, while holding the top sheet. The rod will guide the top layer over the bottom smoothly and evenly without introducing air pockets between the clay layers.

7 Carefully pull the bottom deli sheet away from the clay. Center the burgundy circle over the black clay clock face. Trim the clay from the center hole with the craft knife. Gently lift the tip of one V-section with the craft knife so that it sits in a vertical position. Lift the next V to the left. Press the tip of this V onto the burgundy clay point beneath the first V. Repeat this step going counterclockwise, lifting and pressing each V-section onto the burgundy clay points until the entire circle is complete.

8 Roll out a small piece of pearl clay on the sixth largest setting of the pasta machine. Punch out twelve small circles with the pattern cutter. Roll these into balls and press them over the tip of each arched, gold V.

9 Roll a 14" (36cm) long by ¹/₁₆" (2mm) diameter gold clay snake. Wrap the snake around the burgundy clay circle. Cut off any excess clay and blend the seam with your fingertip. Impress lines into the gold clay every ¹/₈" (3mm) with the tip of a needle tool.

10 Brush a thin layer of liquid polymer clay on the back of the clay baked numbers 12, 3, 6 and 9. Press these numbers into place on the clock face around the black clay border. There should be a ¹/₁₆" (2mm) gap between the numbers and the gold clay border. Apply liquid polymer clay to the back of the remaining numbers and press them into place, spacing them evenly between the first four numbers.

11 Roll out sheets of burgundy and gold clays on the fifth largest setting of the pasta machine. Cut out thirty-six large burgundy teardrops and thirty-six medium gold teardrops with the pattern cutters. Lay a gold teardrop in the center of each burgundy teardrop so that the bottom edges are aligned. Slightly pinch the bottom of each layered teardrop inward.

12 Glue the layered teardrops along the angled edges of the clock. The bottom of each teardrop should sit flush with the bottom edge of the clock. The tips should be facing inward. Bake the clock at 275° F (135° C) for 40 minutes. When cool, attach the clock mechanism, hands and a picture frame hanger.

To help with spacing, place the teardrops in front of each number first. Place two more teardrops between each of the first twelve teardrops, spacing them as evenly as possible.

tip

woven keepsake *box*

*w*eaving is one of the oldest art forms. The beauty of its sheer simplicity is simply timeless. And, of course, we're adapting it for polymer clay! You'll combine this technique with a clever method of constructing a treasure box using nested cookie cutters. This manner of construction takes the guesswork out of assembling sidewalls, lids and bases.

materials

Polymer clay: violet, magenta and pearl

Linen and herringbone rubbing plates (Shade-Tex)

Heart-shaped nested cookie cutters

Flower cutter (Kemper Tools #PC5F)

Large ball-tip stylus

Basic clay kit

1 Roll out two 4" × 4" (10cm × 10cm) sheets of violet and magenta clay on the fourth largest setting of the pasta machine. Spray both sides of each sheet with automotive protectant spray. Spread the spray over the clay with your finger. Lay the sheets facedown over the linen texture rubbing plate. Roll the acrylic rod over the sheets with one firm pass. Lift the clay sheets from the rubbing plate. This will give the clay texture. Cut the clay sheets into ¼" (6mm) wide strips with the clay blade.

2 Roll out a 4" × 4" (10cm × 10cm) square of pearl clay on the largest setting of the pasta machine. Place the clay square on a deli sheet. Cut out a heart from the pearl clay using the largest cutter. Remove the excess clay. Begin your weaving over the pearl clay heart by crossing two violet strips in the center of the heart.

3 Continue weaving in an over and under fashion by adding magenta strips on either side of the top violet strip. Start by raising the bottom of the violet strip and placing the magenta strips underneath. Lay the violet strip back into place. Shift the heart one-half turn. Lift the magenta strips and lay another magenta strip on both sides. Place them under the first magenta strip and over the violet strip in the middle.

4 Continue weaving by adding strips of alternating color, lifting strips so that the clay is woven over and under at each point. Do not weave the strips too closely together. A small square opening should be visible between each intersecting strip. Continue until the pearl clay heart is covered. Press the second largest heart cutter over the center of the woven heart. Remove the excess clay.

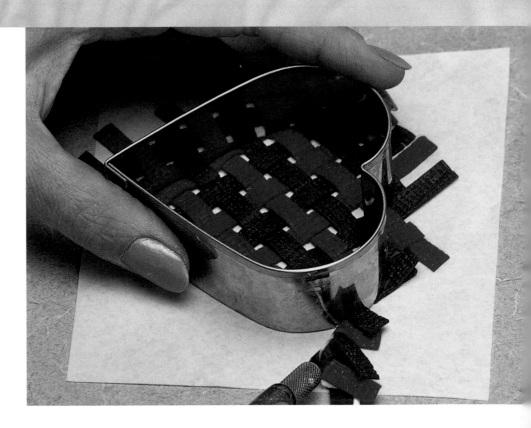

5 Roll out a 10" (25cm) long by ⅛" (3mm) in diameter pearl snake. Wrap the snake around the woven heart and trim any excess clay. Heal the seam with your fingertip. Make diagonal lines every ⅛" (3mm) around the snake with the tip of the needle tool.

6 Roll out a small sheet of pearl clay on the fifth largest setting of the pasta machine. Use the pattern cutter to punch out flowers. Glue a flower in the center of each intersecting violet strip, using polymer clay bonder. Impress the center of each flower with the ball-tip stylus. Bake the woven heart lid on a baking tile at 275º F (135º C) for 30 minutes.

7 While the woven heart is baking, roll out a 10" × 1" (25cm × 3cm) strip of violet clay on the largest setting of the pasta machine. Cut one end at a 45° angle with the clay blade. Starting with the beveled end, wrap the strip around the second largest heart cutter. The edge of the strip should be aligned just under the metal lip at the top of the cutter. Finish the wrapping by cutting off the excess clay at a 45° angle from the opposite direction. Press the beveled ends together and heal the seam with your finger.

8 Spray the violet clay wrapped around the cutter with automotive protectant spray. Spread the spray with your fingers. Emboss the clay with the herringbone rubbing plate. Don't attempt to apply the pattern neatly and evenly. Repeatedly press a corner of the rubbing plate over the clay until a random texture covers the entire strip.

9 After embossing with the herringbone rubbing plate, the clay will have spread. Trim away any excess clay from the bottom and upper lip of the cutter with the clay blade. Bake the wrapped cutter at 275° F (135° C) for 25 minutes.

10 After the violet heart has baked, and while the clay is still warm to the touch, gently loosen it from the cutter by pulling it toward the bottom edge. It may help to wiggle the cutter back and forth while pulling the clay. Continue easing the clay off the cutter until it is removed.

11 Using the largest cutter, cut out another heart from pearl clay that's been rolled out on the largest setting of the pasta machine. Apply polymer clay bonder to the bottom of the cooled violet heart frame and press it over the center of the pearl heart. The frame should be embedded slightly into the pearl heart, leaving a small outer border. Don't overpress, or you'll cut through the base of the box.

Before attempting to slide the violet clay off the cookie cutter, run the tip of the craft knife under the top and bottom edges wherever possible to help loosen the clay. Remove while still cool to the touch. Allowing the clay to completely cool while still on the cutter may result in cracking.

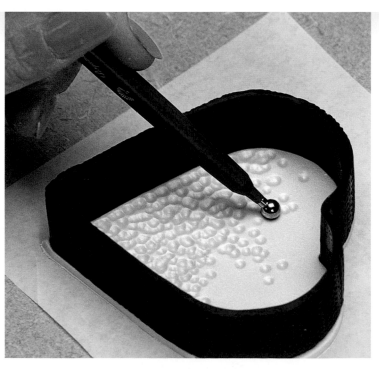

12 Stipple the inside of the box base with the stylus for a finished look.

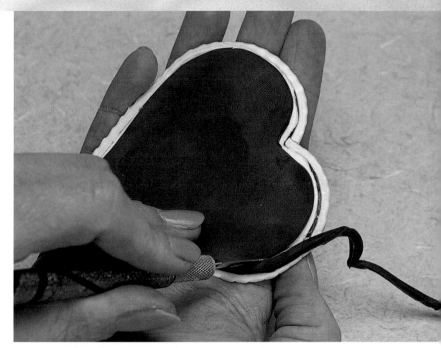

13 Roll out a 10" (25cm) long and ⅛" (3mm) in diameter magenta snake. Glue the snake around the base of the box, using polymer clay bonder. Impress lines around the snake as you did in step 5. Reinsert the second largest cutter halfway into the box sidewalls to help maintain the shape during rebaking. Bake the base at 275º F (135º C) for 35 minutes. While the box base is still warm to the touch, remove the cookie cutter.

14 Using the second largest heart cutter, cut out a heart from a sheet of violet clay rolled out on the largest setting of the pasta machine. Glue it to the bottom of the box lid with polymer clay bonder. Trim ¹/₁₆" (2mm) of clay from the edge of this heart with a craft knife. This interior heart will help hold the lid in place while on the box. Rebake the lid faceup on a deli sheet placed over a baking tile at 275° F (135º C) for 30 minutes.

Gallery Idea

You can come up with a multitude of box ideas using the concepts found in this project. Try using round, oval or square cutters. Play with color combinations when creating woven patterns.

Sutton slice
magnet frame

*P*eople will scratch their heads and wonder at how you created this amazing, two-toned, dual-texture effect developed by my friend Pete Sutton. Like many other great discoveries, this technique was the result of an accident. Pete was looking for a way to streamline the mica shift technique when he discovered this effect. As you might imagine, his attempt didn't produce the results he was looking for, but what he did discover was the beginnings of a fabulous surface treatment you'll use to make these unique frames with matching magnets.

materials

Polymer clay: violet, white and magenta

Adhesive-backed magnetic sheet

Polymer clay texture stamp
(Heart in Hand Studio #LP-SS1)

Heart-shaped nested cookie cutters
(Ateco)

Scissors

Tape

Basic clay kit

1 Roll ¼ block of violet clay through the fourth largest setting of the pasta machine. Spray one side of the clay sheet with automotive protectant spray and spread it over the surface with your fingers. Tear off small pieces of the clay and press it into the stamp with the sprayed surface of the clay touching the stamp. Press the clay firmly with your fingers. Slice off the raised clay with a clean, sharp clay blade (see the tip below). After shaving, the clay should be flush with the top of the stamp, leaving the crevices embedded with clay. Continue adding violet clay and shaving as before, filling an area that is slightly larger than the largest heart cutter. Run the clay blade over the surface of the stamp a few more times to remove any clay residue that may remain on the raised portions of the stamp. If this residue isn't removed, it will adhere to the base layer of clay, and diminish the impact of the pattern.

2 Roll out a sheet of white clay through the third largest setting of the pasta machine. Place the clay over the embedded area of the stamp. Apply automotive protectant spray over the back of the white clay and spread it with your fingers. Press the unsprayed side of the white clay over the embedded area of the stamp. Starting from the center and working your way out toward the edges. Be sure to press the entire surface of the white clay firmly with your fingertips! It's critical that the white clay make firm contact with the embedded clay for this technique to work.

To shave the clay, hold one end of the blade stationary by pressing it against the stamp with an index finger. Carefully pivot the blade with your other hand. This will give you more control. This technique works best with a very sharp blade. Make sure to clean your blade often—even new ones! Residue that causes drag builds up on blades very quickly. This residue can cause the embedded clay to stick to your blade, lifting it out of the stamp. Spray a small puddle of automotive protectant onto your work surface. Dip your fingers into the puddle often to prevent them from sticking to the embedded clay and accidentally lifting it out.

tip

3 Press the small heart into the center of the clay. Make sure to press it firmly against the rubber. Leave the small heart in place. Position the large heart over the small one. The space between the two cutters should be as even as possible all the way around the hearts. Press the large heart down firmly against the stamp. With the cookie cutters still in place, bake the stamp at 275º F (135º C) for 15 minutes. A slight odor is not unusual when the rubber gets warm. Don't worry, the stamp won't burn!

4 Once the clay has cooled, remove the cookie cutters from the clay. Gently bend and pull the stamp away from the clay. If any violet clay remains embedded in the stamp, carefully remove it with a pair of tweezers and reattach it to the base layer, using polymer clay bonder. Place the clay facedown on a tile. Cut through the outlines left by the cutters, using the craft knife. Separate the two hearts.

Select a large and small cookie cutter to determine the size of your frame and photo opening. The difference between the large and small frame should measure at least ¾" (19mm) wide or larger.

5 Roll out two magenta clay snakes. One should be 12" (30cm) long and ⅛" (3mm) in diameter, the other 6" (15cm) long and ¹⁄₁₆" (2mm) in diameter. Attach the wider snake around the outer edge of the heart frame with polymer clay bonder. Repeat this step on the inside of the frame with the narrow snake. Trim away the excess clay and blend the seams with your fingers.

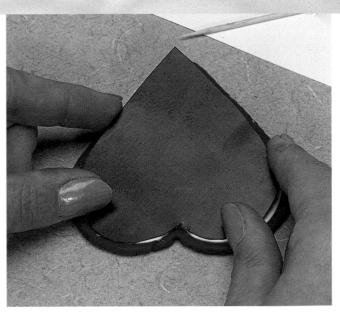

6 Glue a 7" (18cm) long by ⅛" (3mm) diameter magenta snake around the smaller center heart removed from the frame. Make diagonal impressions every ⅛" (3mm) with the needle tool on all the magenta borders for a ropelike effect. Rebake the hearts on a tile at 275º F (135º C) for 25 minutes.

7 Use the cutters as a template for cutting both the magnetic backing and the photo. Position the large cutter over your picture. Trace along the inside edge of the cutter with a pen, and trim the photo ⅛" (3mm) in from the pen line. Repeat the tracing step for the magnet, but cut directly along the pen line. Tape the photo in place over the back of the frame. Peel the backing off the magnet. Glue the tacky side to the back of the frame with two-part epoxy. Repeat the tracing and gluing steps to finish the matching magnet.

Gallery Ideas

Use a variety of clays and different stamp patterns to make your frames and magnets. It's best to use an unmounted stamp that has both detail and depth. This technique will not work with shallow or too finely detailed stamps. Explore the magic of contrast by playing with different color combinations. A wonderful effect is created by embedding the stamp with several hues of clay from the same color family.

pinecone
bowl

*S*calloping and layering combine to create a sumptu-
ous vessel that subtly invokes the image of a pinecone.
This bowl is the perfect container for potpourri, trinkets,
wrapped candy and more. Whether the décor is warm
and woodsy or classically contemporary, this artful piece
will dress up any interior.

materials

Polymer clay: copper and 2 blocks of black

Liquid polymer clay

Rose bowl (Anchor Hocking #3354)

Large ball-tip stylus

2¼" (6cm) circle cutter or template

Texturing tool (retractable ballpoint pen or dedicated cake decorating tip)

Teardrop pattern cutter (Kemper Tools #PCAT)

Circle pattern cutter (Kemper Tools #PC5C)

Knitting needle

Basic clay kit

1 Cut a 2¼" (6cm) diameter clay circle from copper clay that has been rolled out on the largest setting of the pasta machine. Press the bottom of the rose bowl over the copper circle and trim away the excess clay, leaving only the bottom covered. Texture the copper clay with the tip of the stylus, then cut away excess clay from the bottom edge of the bowl with the clay blade.

2 Cut out thirteen small copper teardrops from clay that's been run through the fifth largest setting of the pasta machine. Cut out fifty-two large teardrops from black clay that's been rolled out on the fourth largest setting of the pasta machine. Layer the copper teardrops over the center of thirteen black clay teardrops. Start the first row of the bowl by placing the thirteen copper and black layered teardrops against the glass with the pointed end up. The placement should begin 1" (25mm) below the bowl's rim. The copper teardrops should be against the glass. When you finish the first row, bend the upper third of each teardrop away from the glass. Press the tip of the teardrop into the black clay to secure the loop.

3 Pinch the tips of the remaining thirty-nine black teardrops between your thumb and index finger.

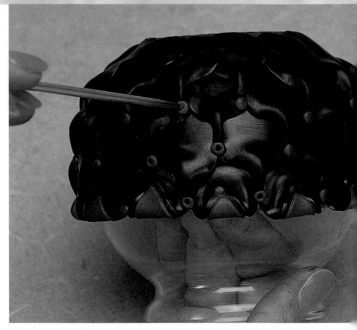

4 Place each pinched teardrop, with the pointed end up, in between and halfway up the teardrops of the first row. Be sure to press the tip down onto the previous row of teardrops so that it adheres to the clay above it. Continue until the second row is complete, stretching or compressing the last few teardrops only as needed. Finish the last two rows in the same manner. Since the bowl is narrower toward the bottom, it will be necessary to slightly overlap each teardrop over the one placed before it. For the last row, the bottom of each teardrop should be aligned flush with the copper clay bottom of the bowl.

5 Roll out a sheet of copper clay on the third largest setting of the pasta machine. Punch out several dozen copper circles, using the tiny pattern cutter. Roll these circles into balls. Use polymer clay bonder applied with a toothpick to attach a copper ball over the tip of each pinched leaf. Do not place copper balls over the tips on the folded teardrops of the first row. Press the tip of a knitting needle into the center of each copper ball to decorate and secure the clays together.

6 Turn the bowl upside down. Roll a large pinch of copper clay through the largest setting on the pasta machine. Cut out three large teardrops of copper clay. Roll each teardrop into a ball. Use the needle tool to mark three evenly spaced spots on the bottom of the bowl. Use a toothpick to apply a small ring of liquid polymer clay around each mark. Without touching the liquid polymer clay, put a small drop of polymer clay bonder in the center of the liquid clay rings. Press the copper balls over the glue and liquid polymer clay. Allow the polymer clay bonder to cure for a minute.

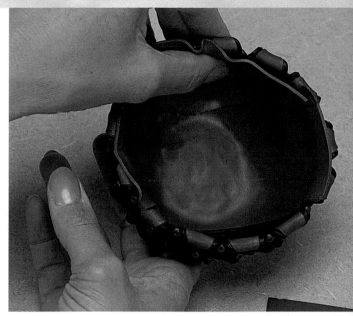

7 Turn the bowl over and place it on a deli sheet over a baking tile. Gently press the bowl down to slightly flatten the feet. With the bowl resting on a level surface, bend down so that your line of vision is eye level with the bowl to make sure the bowl is level. Press the rim of the bowl if necessary to adjust the level. Carefully lift the bowl away from the deli sheet and bake it upside down on a tile at 275° F (135° C) for 40 minutes. While the bowl is slightly warm to the touch, gently pry the clay away from the glass bowl. Rotate the bowl often while loosening. Continue until the clay separates from the glass. When cool, roll out a 3" × 8" (4cm × 20cm) sheet of copper clay on the fourth largest setting of the pasta machine. Place the sheet in the inside center of the bowl, pressing it against the base and sides with your fingers.

8 Roll out a 6" × 6" (15cm × 15cm) sheet of copper clay on the fourth largest setting of the pasta machine. Cut out a circle from this sheet with the craft knife. Neatness doesn't count here. Stretch the circle with your hands into an oval shape and cut it in half lengthwise with the clay blade. Place each half over the exposed inner walls of the bowl, stretching if necessary to make contact with the copper clay strip in the center. Blend the seams of the patched clay sheets with your fingertips.

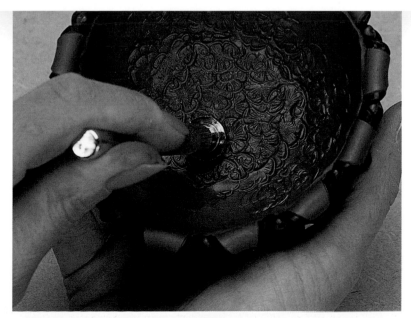

Trying to pry cooled clay away from the glass bowl may result in cracking since the clay will shrink slightly when it cools. If the bowl has cooled, insert it back in the oven for about a minute and repeat the steps to remove it from the glass form while it is still warm. Never try to remove the clay while it is still hot!

9 Texture the entire inner surface of the bowl with the texture tool. Rebake the bowl, standing upright in a 275° F (135° C) oven for 20 minutes.

anytime *gifts*

*i*f you need a gift for a special occasion, you've come to the right place. Here's a collection of projects that are perfect to make for holidays, birthdays, anniversaries, graduations, weddings, new babies or to tell someone special how much you care. These gifts lend themselves to variation, making it easy to customize your gift for anyone you know. Just follow the simple steps for sculpting, laminating, texturing, stamping and embellishing your way to the perfect anytime gift.

projects

celebration
toasting goblet

*C*elebrations are the cornerstone
of our lives. We use them to mark
the things that mean the most to
us. Weddings and anniversaries
are among the most cherished
and fêted occasions we can
share. What better way to
toast one of life's most
important moments than
with a special goblet?
Whether it's a celebration
for two or two hundred, these
stunning goblets will set off
the moment with great style.
Learn the simple steps to create
polymer clay "ribbon" roses and
adornments to create a gift made
for romance.

materials

Polymer clay: gold and pearl

Inexpensive champagne flutes or wineglasses

Circle pattern cutter

Paintbrush

Large ball-tip stylus

Clay gun with 3mm circle disc

Teardrop pattern cutters
(Kemper Tools medium #PC1T, small #PC2T)

Basic clay kit

1 Roll out a 4" x 4" (10cm x 10cm) square of pearl clay on the third largest setting of the pasta machine. Place the base of the glass over the clay. Cut around the base of the glass with a craft knife. Remove the excess clay and lift away the glass.

2 Punch out and remove the center of the clay circle with the circle pattern cutter. Cut a straight line through the circle, rom the center to the edge. This creates a collar. Brush polymer clay bonder onto the base of the glass and wrap the clay collar over the goblet's base. Press the clay onto the base to work out any trapped air.

3 Stipple the entire clay base with the stylus.

To make a pair of even more distinctive goblets, reverse the use of gold and pearl clays for the bases and flowers to make each one truly unique and easily distinguishable from the other.

tip

4 Load the clay gun with very warm and soft pearl clay. Extrude one 24" (61cm) and one 16" (41cm) long snake. Reload the gun if necessary. Repeat this step using gold clay. Place the 24" (61cm) pearl and gold snakes side by side. Glue these snakes around the stem of the goblet with polymer clay bonder. Wind them, side by side, up the stem. Stop where the stem reaches the bowl of the goblet. Trim away the excess clay at an angle for a more refined line.

 tip While it's helpful to have several clay guns for different colors, it can be costly to have one for every color! An easy way to clean a gun between uses is to bake the gun and plunger at 275° F (135° C) for 5 minutes. When the gun is cool, pick off the hardened clay with a needle tool. If you need a few more tips on getting the most out of your clay gun, turn to pages 19 and 72.

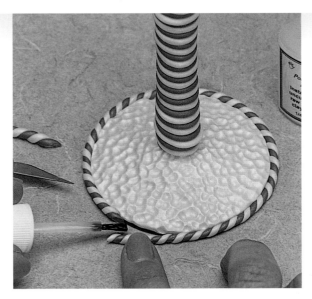

5 Place the 16" (41cm) pearl and gold snakes side by side and twist along the entire length. Glue the twisted clay around the base of the goblet with polymer clay bonder.

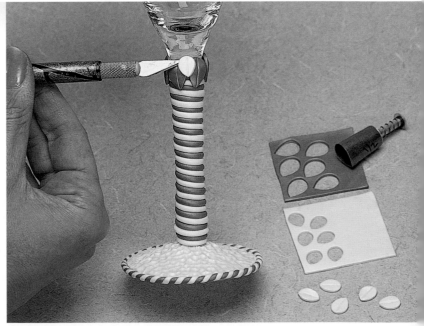

6 Cut out six large gold teardrops from a small sheet of clay rolled out on the fourth largest setting of the pasta machine. Impress a vertical line down the center of each teardrop. Repeat this step with pearl clay, using the smaller teardrop cutter. Press the gold teardrops evenly around the clay twist at the top of the stem. Press the six smaller pearl teardrops between the gold teardrops at the point at the top of the stem.

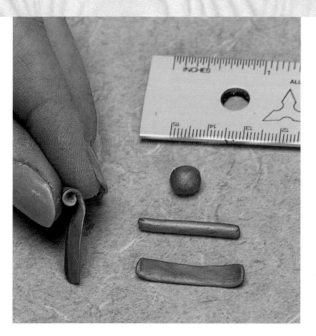

7 Roll several dozen small balls of gold clay, ³⁄₈"–¹⁄₄" (3mm–6mm) in diameter. Roll one ball into a small snake about 1" (25mm) long and flatten it between your fingers. Roll the flattened snake, jelly roll style, to form a rosebud. Pinch and shape the edges with your fingers. Repeat this step to make ten rosebuds, setting four aside.

8 Flatten the remaining gold balls between your thumb and index finger to make petals. Create roses by wrapping three to five petals around six of the rosebuds.

9 Roll the bases of each flower between your thumb and index finger to form a pointed cone. Slice off the cone end near the base of each flower.

An alternative to placing the roses, leaves and ribbons randomly around the base of the goblet is to make an arrangement at one point of the base. This creates a central focus point and a "front" of each goblet.

tip

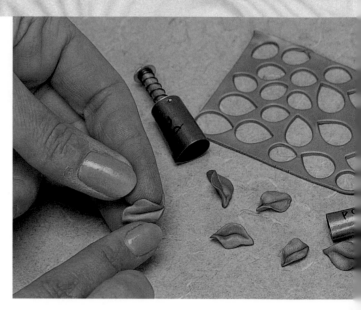

10 Insert the needle tool into the center of the rosebuds to handle them while placing and gluing them to the base of the goblet. Use polymer clay bonder to secure the rosebuds.

11 Roll out a sheet of gold clay on the fourth largest setting of the pasta machine. Cut out several dozen large and small teardrop shapes. Slightly fold each teardrop shape in half along its length. Pinch along the fold to form a vein. Carefully pull the halves apart. Bend and pinch the sides of the leaves and tips to shape.

12 Glue one or two leaves at the base of each flower as desired.

13 Roll out pearl clay on the fifth largest setting of the pasta machine. Cut several strips 1"–3" (3cm–8cm) in length by ⅛" (3mm) wide. Twist the strips to make ribbons. Place them randomly among the leaves and flowers. Use the stylus to press the ribbon ends onto the clay base to secure. Repeat the steps above to make the second goblet. Bake goblets at 275º F (135º C) for 35 minutes and allow to cool before using.

TO CARE FOR THE GOBLETS

Hand wash the glass portion of the goblet using warm, sudsy water and a nonabrasive sponge or cloth. Dry immediately after washing. Do not leave immersed in water or place in a dishwasher.

Gallery Ideas

Why make decorative stemware for only special occasions? How about dressing up inexpensive stemware with brightly colored clays? Decorate the bases using cut outs made from a clay cutter, or embellishments like polka dots and squiggles. Use these fun and funky glasses every day. Why not make life more elegant and use these glasses for juice and milk? This festive stemware is a great way for your guests to tell their glass from all the others!

ancestral
photo box

*m*emories are our most cherished possession. Photographs are a
wonderful way to preserve the memory of generations past. This project
features a unique method of permanently transferring these cherished
images to clay. The best part is that you don't have to sacrifice your
original photo to create this incredible project. You'll have the benefit
of preserving your treasured photos for future generations while creating
a lovely keepsake to give as a gift or keep for yourself.

materials

Polymer clay: gold and 2 blocks of brown

Liquid polymer clay

Beige acid-free photo box

Color photocopies or scanned inkjet prints of selected photos (do not use actual photographs as these will not be bakeable)

12" (30cm) of 1" (25mm) wide lace

Metallic inks: bronze, copper and gold (Ranger)

Love letter stamp (Heart in Hand Studio #LP-LL2)

Gold pigment ink (Ranger)

Perfect Pearls mica powder: Sunflower Sparkle (Ranger)

Paper plate

Sea sponge

Oval nested cookie cutters (Ateco)

Heat gun

Flat paintbrush

Round craft brush

Adhesive tape

Basic clay kit

1 Pour a small amount of the metallic inks onto a paper plate. Wet the sea sponge and squeeze out any excess water, then dip the sponge into one of the inks. Blot the sponge over the sides of the box and lid, reloading the sponge as needed. When you've covered the box to your satisfaction, allow the box to dry for a few minutes. Rinse the sponge and repeat this step with the remaining two inks. Do not cover the box completely with ink. The beige color should show through in spots.

2 Determine the number of photos you wish to showcase on your box. Select the cutter sizes you will be using to create your openings. Use the cutters as templates to determine whether the image needs to be reduced or enlarged when printing. Keep in mind that the photo opening will be slightly smaller than the interior edges of your cutter since a clay border will be added later.

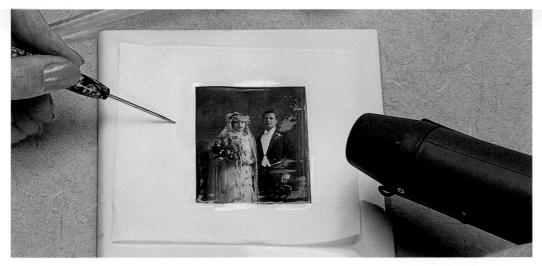

Do not hold the heat gun closer than ½"–5" (10cm–13cm) away from the image or burning may occur. Keep the heat gun moving at all times when curing the liquid medium.

tip

3 Trim the copied photos into rectangles or squares. It's important to have at least a ½" (13mm) border of paper beyond the portion of the photo that will be visible. Brush a thin layer of liquid polymer clay over the front of each photo. Cure the clay with the heat gun. When the high gloss of the liquid polymer turns to a satiny sheen, the clay is cured. Allow the paper to cool for 1 minute. Repeat this step on the back of the photo. The air from the heat gun tends to cause pooling along the paper edges. After cooling, trim ¼" (6mm) away from the photo edges. Set the photos aside.

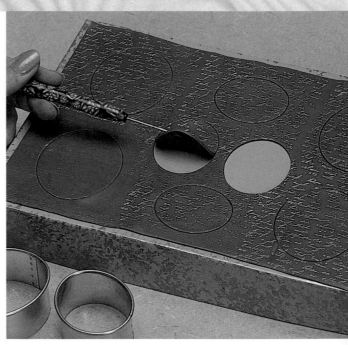

4 Make three 4" x 8" (10cm x 20cm) sheets of brown clay rolled through the third largest setting of the pasta machine. Cut a beveled edge along one length of two sheets, and along both lengths of the third sheet. Assemble the beveled clay over a sheet of waxed paper. Ink the letter stamp with the gold ink. Press the stamp in the upper left-hand corner of the clay sheet. Use enough pressure to leave a shallow impression. Reink and stamp the clay until you cover the remaining two panels.

5 Carefully lift the clay sheet off the waxed paper and place it on the lid of the box. Use the oval cutters to make the photo openings in the stamped clay. Turn the box upside down, and place the lid over the base of the box. Bake the lid and the box bottom together at 275º F (135º C) for 30 minutes. This will prevent the lid from bowing inward during baking.

Need some help assembling the sheets of brown clay? Follow the instructions for step 6 of the Faux Tortoiseshell Change Caddy on page 36.

6 Once the lid has cooled, carefully slide the clay blade underneath the baked clay on all four sides. Lift the clay off the lid of the box. Tape the laminated pictures to the back of the clay frame panel. When all the photos are in place, glue the clay photo panel to the lid, using two-part epoxy. Make sure the panel is centered on the box before the glue sets.

7 Roll out a ½ block of gold clay through the fourth largest setting of the pasta machine. Cut the clay lengthwise into four 1½" (4cm) wide strips. Trim two strips to 8" (20cm) long. Trim the other two strips to 11½" (29cm) long. Place the lace over one clay strip. Roll the acrylic rod over the length of the lace, embedding it into the clay. While the lace is still in place, brush gold mica powder onto the exposed areas of the clay strip. Pull the lace off of the powdered strip. Repeat this step with the remaining three strips.

8 Use the craft knife to trim the edges of the clay strips, making them straight and even. If your lace pattern has a scalloped edge, you may wish to trim the outer edge, following the impressed outline.

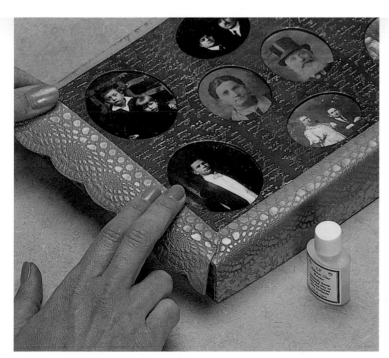

9 Glue the lace clay borders to the box lid with polymer clay bonder. The strips should slightly overlap the outer edge of the stamped clay panel. Miter or cut the corners at a 45° angle.

10 Roll a ⅛" (3mm) diameter snake, 8"–12" (20cm–30cm) in length, for each photo. Glue these snakes around the opening of each photo. Trim the excess clay, and seal the seam with your finger. Impress diagonal lines around each snake approximately every ⅛" (3mm) with the tip of the needle tool. Brush another thin layer of liquid polymer clay over each photo. Bake the box lid at 275° F (135° C) for 30 minutes as you did in step 5. In the unlikely event the panel becomes loose from the lid, reattach it with two-part epoxy.

bowed
gift tin

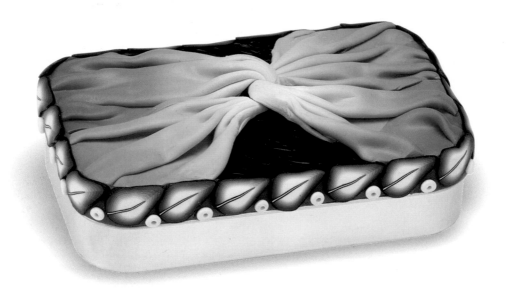

*m*int tins are easy to come by and are available in a variety of shapes and sizes. This project features the common rectangular tins, but can be easily adapted to other shapes and sizes. The gathered clay bow is the focal point of this lovely container that also features millefiori caning and textured layers. The finished tin is a handy vessel for refilling with mints or other treats. It's also ideal for storing small treasures such as jewelry or photos.

Polymer clay: black, magenta, blue and white

New or recycled mint tin, approximately 2¼" x 3¾" (6cm x 10cm) or larger

Squiggles rubbing plate (Shade Tex #SH-P-8)

Circle pattern cutter (Kemper Tools #PCR5)

Basic clay kit

Some tins have numbers imprinted on the sides. Remove these with a cotton ball saturated with acetone-based nail polish remover.

tip

1   To help the clay adhere to the tin, roughen the tin's surface with the needle tool. Roll a 3" x 4" (8cm x 10cm) sheet of black clay through the second largest setting of the pasta machine. Spray the clay with automotive protectant spray. Place the treated clay facedown over the squiggle rubbing plate. Roll the clay and the texture sheet together through the third largest setting of the pasta machine. Cut the rubbing sheet in half if necessary to fit it through the pasta machine. Peel the clay away from the texture plate and glue the clay to the top of the tin with polymer clay bonder. Make sure there are no air bubbles between the clay and tin. Cut away the excess clay from the tin's edges with the clay blade.

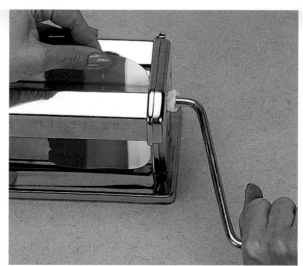

2   Roll a 10" (25cm) long by ⅜" (10mm) wide snake of magenta clay through the fifth largest setting of the pasta machine. Cut a straight edge along one side of the flattened magenta clay. Wrap the clay around the tin's lid with the straight side sitting flush with the edges of the lid. Trim away any excess clay after wrapping and blend the seams together with your finger.

3   Make a narrow-width, approximately 1½" (4cm) wide, Skinner blend sheet using blue and white clay. Do not roll the sheet into a cane. During this project make sure you run the sheet through the rollers in the same direction used during the blending process.

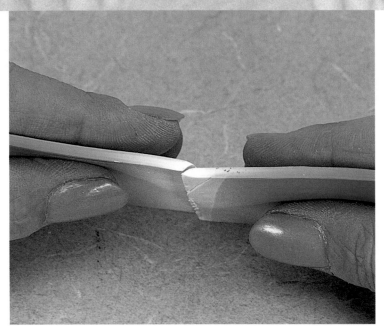

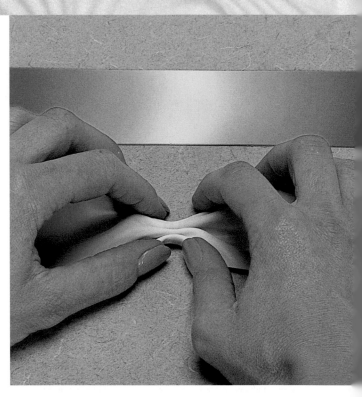

4 Cut the narrow-width Skinner blend in half lengthwise. Slightly trim the white edges, holding the clay blade at an angle, creating beveled edges. Flip one half of the sheet over and butt the beveled edges of the white ends together to form a single sheet that graduates from blue to white to blue. Spray the clay sheets with a small amount of automotive protectant spray. Blend the seams together by rolling with the acrylic rod. Repeat steps 3 and 4 with magenta and white clay.

5 Roll each Skinner blended strip widthwise through the fifth largest setting of the pasta machine. Gather the clay sheets at the center, creating several folds with your fingers.

To narrow the length of the pasta machine rollers, cut a 2" (5cm) long section from a 1" (25mm) diameter wood dowel. Place the dowel against one end of the machine rollers. The dowel will prevent the blended sheet from spreading the entire length of the rollers and keep it narrow. Leave the dowel in place when stretching the graded sheet. For this project, do not turn the sheet while you are thinning it.

6 Cross one sheet diagonally over the other. Place a drop of polymer clay bonder in the center of the black textured clay and lay the crossed sections over the tin's lid. Lift each clay strip at the corners and glue them to the black clay. Lightly press the clay over and around the corners of the lid. Trim the excess clay with the clay blade. You may also twist the gathered strips together at the center for a variation on the blended bow.

7 Cut a 1" (25mm) section from a blue/white Skinner blend cane. Cut this section in half with a clean, sharp clay blade. Sandwich a 1" x ½" (25mm x 13mm) piece of white clay rolled through the third largest setting of the pasta machine between two same-size sheets of black clay that have been rolled out on the fifth largest setting of the pasta machine. Place the sandwiched sheet halfway across the diameter of the divided cane. Piece the two halves back together to create a vein in the center of the cane. Wrap the cane with a sheet of black clay that's been rolled through the sixth largest setting of the pasta machine. Compress, roll and reduce the cane to ½" (13mm) in diameter. Pinch the cane along the top length between your thumb and forefinger. The vein should be pointing upward.

8 Cut several dozen slices from the cane. Glue these end to end along the clay-covered edges of the tin with polymer clay bonder.

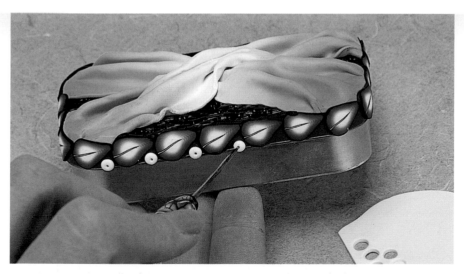

9 Roll a small sheet of white clay through the fourth largest setting of the pasta machine. Punch out several white clay circles with the pattern cutter. Roll the circles into balls. Use a toothpick to apply a small dot of polymer clay bonder over the opening between the bottom of each cane slice. Press the white clay balls over the adhesive. Insert the needle tool through the center of each ball to secure and decorate. Bake the tin at 275° F (135° C) for 35 minutes.

A small charm or crystal may be added to the center of the bow for added flair.

tip

translucent
transfer votive

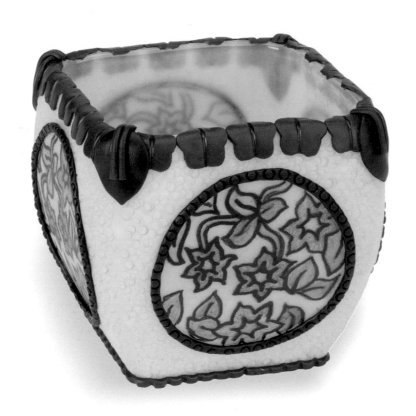

*C*ast a romantic glow in any room with this delicately hued votive holder. Soft luminescent shadows radiate through the translucent floral pattern surrounding the holder. A subtle Asian motif mixes with an invitingly textured surface. Learn an unique image transfer technique to create this elegant project.

materials

Polymer clay: 1 block of black, translucent and red

Square glass candle votive

Colored pencils (PrismaColor)

2¼" (6cm) circle cookie cutter

Black fine-tip permanent marker

Retractable ballpoint pen

Flower pattern cutter
(Kemper Tools #PCAF)

Teardrop pattern cutter
(Kemper Tools #PCBT)

Basic clay kit

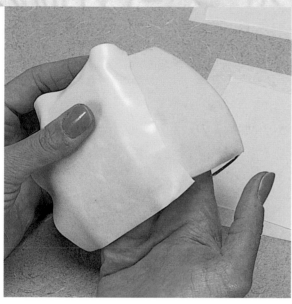

1 Roll out four 4" x 4" (10cm x 10cm) sheets of translucent polymer clay on the sixth largest setting of the pasta machine. Place one sheet at a time over each of the four panels on the votive. Work out any trapped air by pressing it out to the edges, or piercing the clay with the craft knife and blending the hole back together with your fingertip. Trim the excess clay from the edges of each panel before adding another. Blend the seams together with your fingers.

2 Press the blunt side of the circle cookie cutter into the center of the four clay-covered sides of the votive, leaving an indentation. Trace the flower pattern on page 111 or your own design onto the waxed side of four deli sheets, using the permanent marker and the cookie cutter to determine the size of the pattern. Color in the flowers and leaves with colored pencils of your choice. Cut the colored circles out with scissors. Place each transfer facedown over the centers of each side of the votive. Burnish the transfers onto the clay by rubbing your fingers back and forth for 30 seconds each transfer and leave the deli sheets in place on the clay.

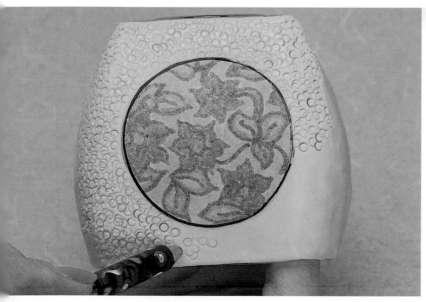

3 Texture the translucent clay surrounding the transfer sheet with the tip of the ballpoint pen with the ink cartridge retracted.

4 Blend a small pinch of black clay with a ¼ block of red clay to create burgundy-colored clay.

5 Roll the burgundy clay out on the fifth largest setting of the pasta machine. Cut out twenty flowers, using the pattern cutter. Bend five flowers over the edges of the votive on all four sides. Make a vertical indentation through the middle of each flower by pressing with the needle tool.

6 Cut out four teardrop shapes from black clay rolled through the fourth largest setting of the pasta machine. Press a teardrop (pointed end down) over each corner of the votive.

7 Roll a 1/16" (2mm) diameter and 8" (20cm) long snake of burgundy clay. Cut eight 3/4" (19mm) sections. Place two sections side by side. Press each double section down over the center of each black teardrop, starting at the top of the teardrop.

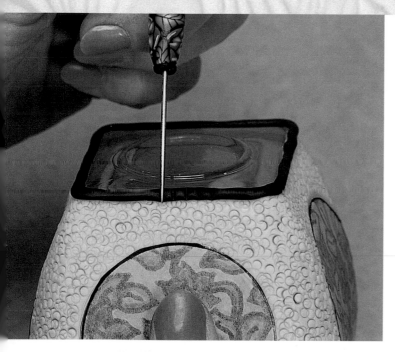

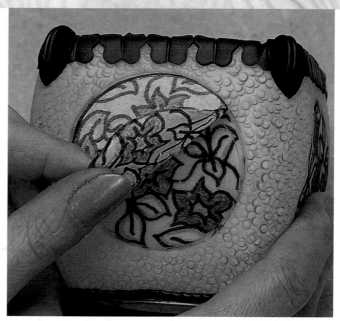

8 Roll a 10" x ⅛" (25cm x 3mm) snake of burgundy clay and wrap it around the bottom of the votive, using polymer clay bonder. Press vertical lines along the snake every ⅛" (3mm) with the tip of the needle tool. With the deli sheet transfers in place, bake the votive at 275° F (135° C) for 30 minutes.

9 When the votive has cooled, peel off the deli sheets to reveal the transfers.

10 Roll four 10" x 1/16" (25cm x 2mm) diameter black clay snakes. Use polymer clay bonder to glue the snakes around the circular impressions made with the blunt edge of the circle cutter. Trim the excess clay. Impress the black clay borders every ⅛" (3mm) using the retracted end of the pen. Rebake the votive at 275° F (135° C) for 30 minutes.

Use this pattern for the Translucent Transfer Votive. Enlarge or reduce as necessary.

powder inlay
tag book

*U*sing shipping tags is a fun and easy way to make miniature books. Let your imagination run free when creating your master-piece. Make a diminutive diary, a petite photo album or a clever coupon book. This project makes the perfect gift for someone who has everything. Learn how to transfer resin-based mica powders onto polymer clay in a pattern.

materials

Polymer clay: black and copper

Eleven shipping tags

Perfect Pearls mica powder, Perfect Bronze (Ranger)

Copper polymer clay foil

Acrylic sealer or floor finish

Metallic gold-tone jewelry or scrapbook embellishments

8" (20cm) of ½"–1" (13mm–25mm) wide gold wired ribbon

Tumbling leaves texture stamp (Heart in Hand Studio #LP-TL1)

Flower stamp (Leather Factory #D617)

Natural hair paintbrush

Circle pattern cutter (Kemper Tools #PC4R)

Basic clay kit

1 Complete all the steps of this project on a work tile to prevent the clay from stretching. Dip the brush into the mica powder. Gently tap the brush on the rim of the container to shake off excess powder. This is necessary to prevent powder from falling into the stamp's crevices. Brush the raised portion of the tumbling leaves texture stamp with the powder. Repeat loading the brush and applying powder until a generous coat of powder covers the raised area of the stamp.

2 Roll out two 2½" x 5" (6cm x 13cm) sheets of black polymer clay on the third largest setting of the pasta machine. Spray one side of each sheet with automotive protectant spray. Carefully place the unsprayed surface of one clay sheet over the powdered stamp. The clay cannot be moved or repositioned after it has been set on the stamp. Roll the acrylic rod over the clay sheet, lightly and in one pass only! Remove the clay and repeat loading the stamp with powder and embossing the second clay sheet as above.

3 Place one of the tags over the embossed clay sheet. Trim the excess clay away from the sides. Cut out the clay from the top-center hole in the tag with the craft knife.

4 To make a striped cane, roll a 1½" (4cm) long by ¾" (19mm) diameter copper snake. Cut five ⅛" (3mm) strips from a 1½" x 1" (38mm x 25mm) sheet of black clay, rolled through the fourth largest setting of the pasta machine. Place the strips around the copper snake, leaving some space between each strip.

5 Roll and reduce the snake to 3" (8cm) long and cut it in half. Roll one half to 16" (41cm) long, about ³⁄₈" (10mm) in diameter, then twist the snake along its entire length. Repeat this step with the other striped cane.

6 Glue the snake around the outside of the clay tag, using polymer clay bonder. Apply glue in 1"–2" (3cm–5cm) sections at a time. Trim away the excess clay. Repeat this step using the other snake and tag.

Even when applied sparingly, polymer clay bonder may seep between the clay tag and the rope border, and onto the tile. If this should occur, carefully slide the clay blade under each tag to loosen them after the tags have been baked and cooled.

7 Burnish a 2" x 2" (5cm x 5cm) piece of copper polymer clay foil onto a square of black clay that has been rolled through the fourth largest setting of the pasta machine. Place the clay on a ceramic tile. See pages 15 and 18 for tips on burnishing. Make two to three dozen impressions in the foiled clay with the leather flower stamp. Cut out each impression with the circle pattern cutter. Lift away the excess clay. Slide the clay blade under the foiled clay flowers to lift them from the tile.

9   Decorate the ten interior tags as desired and sandwich them between the two clay tags. Cut one end of the wired ribbon at an angle. Thread the wire through the clay covers and tags. Tie into a bow and trim the excess ribbon as needed.

8   Decorate the clay cover for the book. Press an embellishment onto the center of one of the tags. Glue foiled flowers over the intersection area between each leaf box in the pattern. Glue extra flowers around the center embellishment to hold it in place. Bake the clay covers at 275º F (135º C) for 30 minutes. Reattach the embellishment with epoxy after baking.

tip   When adding the flowers, brush a drop of polymer clay bonder onto the tip of a toothpick and apply it to the clay. This will keep the powder on the clay from contaminating the glue brush and give you more control over how much glue you apply.

Gallery Ideas

The joy of tag books! Try to find stamps that mirror the theme of your tag books, and use coordinating colors of clay for them. Embellishments can also identify the theme of the book.

gallery

Cocker spaniel magnet by Stephanie Rutz

This highly detailed cocker spaniel magnet is a specialty of the artist who is fairly new to the medium.

Desert scene millefiori votive by Rhonda Garlick

The desert landscape is represented in vibrant detail through this millefiori appliqué votive.

Banner necklace by Karin Serra

This Asian transfer pendant strung with beads has the look of an ancient artifact.

"Meadow Fae" sculpture by Kathy Davis

Meadow Fae is one of this accomplished artist's fairy dolls. Photo by Kathy Davis.

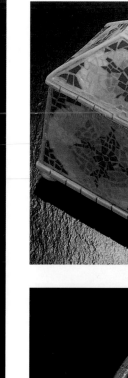

Treasure Box by Irene Yurkewych

This mosaic treasure box features six shades of faux amber that can be found throughout nature.

Leaf necklace by Jill Ackiron-Moses

This elegant teardrop necklace features graduated elements that fuse a rich symmetry of color and pattern together with clay.

gallery

Asian accordion journal by Lisa Pavelka

This Asian collage journal features stamped elements along with clay, pearl and Mizuhiki embellishments.

"Bull's Eye" pendant by Lisa Pavelka

The millefiori cabochon pendant is surrounded by a stippled black clay border and set in a custom sterling bezel.

Flower pins by Deborah Anderson

Shaped and inlayed millefiori cane slices come together in this stunning trio of flower pins. Photo by Liv Ames.

Silk screened pillow bead pendant with dichroic glass by Lisa Pavelka

This pillow bead pendant features dual layer silk screening on clay with a clay bezel and dichroic glass accent beads.

Patchwork Mokumé Gané rabbit sculpture by Lisa Pavelka

This rabbit sculpture is covered with a patchwork veneer of mokumé gané and marbled clay squares.

gallery

Navajo-pattern millefiori bracelet by Kim Cavender

The look of an elaborate Navajo rug pattern is captured with this shifted millefiori sectional bracelet.

Angel Doll by Regina Edmonds

This delicate fairy is small enough to fit into a teacup. The talented artist hand sculpts these one-of-a-kind treasures.

Sterling silver and millefiori bracelet by Judy Belcher

These intricately detailed, domed millefiori squares form an exquisite bracelet when strung with crystals and sterling silver components.

Polymer clay angel pin by Samantha Katz

This angel pin/magnet features a combination of both simple and complex millefiori cane designs.

Quilted polymer clay evening bag by Judy Belcher

This quilted purse is actually polymer clay that's been sewn, a dicovery made by the artist. After testing all brands of polymer clay, Kato Polyclay was found to be the only one that can be sewn with a machine. No special needle was required.

Dimensional millefiori bead bracelet by Kim Cavender

This cheerful bracelet is made from dimensional millefiori cane slices and elements mounted on oval clay cabochons and strung with sterling silver components.

gallery

"Art Unraveled" Asian triptych polymer clay collage by Lisa Pavelka

This Asian triptych is composed of both clay and non-clay embellishments assembled in a collage style.

"A Walk in the Garden" polymer clay shoe by Lisa Pavelka

This shoe was created for the "Feet of Clay" artist design challenge sponsored by Kato Polyclay. It features faux hand sticking and quilting with clay, patterned foil inlay and dimensional millefiori flowers.

"I Love a Mystery" teapot from the Breland collection by Lisa Pavelka

This teapot is a functional piece that is the third in an ongoing series commissioned by the Breland collection.

Faux carved fossilized Ivory pendant by Johnny Kuborssy

The look of fossilized ivory is captured in this pendant featuring petroglyph style carvings.

Geisha vessel by Dotty McMillan

This hand sculpted Geisha vessel offers a stunning perspective of Asian style.

Razberi Kidz™ millefiori heart pendant by Julie Wise

The whimsical faces grace the front of this heart-shaped pendant polished to a glass-like finish.

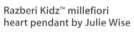

Fan brooch by Lisa Pavelka

This stylized fan brooch features antiqued stamping and image transfer techniques.

resources

Organizations

National Polymer Clay Guild
Web site: www.npcg.org
National organization dedicated to polymer clay education

Society of Craft Designers
(740) 452-4541
Web site: www.craftdesigners.org
Organization supporting professional craft designers for the craft and hobby industries

Publications

The Crafts Report
Telephone: (800) 777-7098
Web site: www.craftsreport.com
Monthly magazine devoted to the hobby-for-profit and professional crafter

Jewelry Crafts
Telephone: (800) 528-1024
Web site: www.jewelrycrafts@mag.com
Bimonthly magazine featuring many polymer clay projects

Lapidary Journal
Telephone: (800) 676-4336
Web site: www.lapidaryjournal.com
Monthly jewelry and gem magazine

Polymer Café Magazine
Telephone: (678) 380-5783
Web site: www.polymercafe.com
Magazine for polymer clay enthusiasts

Suppliers

Accent Import—fimozone.com
Telephone: (800) 989-2889
Fax: (702) 891-9695
Web site: www.fimozone.com
Fimo polymer clays, tools and accessories

Alumicolor
Telephone: (800) 624-9379
Fax: (970) 282-7100
Web site: www.alumicolor.com
Rulers and measuring tools

American Art Clay Co., Inc. (AMACO)
Telephone: (800) 374-1600
Web site: www.amaco.com
Fimo Classic, Fimo Soft, gold leaf, WireForm, ArtEmboss metal sheets, clay blades, millefiori canes, molds, tools and polymer clay accessories

Anchor Hocking Consumer Glass Company
Telephone: (740) 681-6478
Fax: (740) 681-6040
Web site: www.anchorhocking.com
Rose bowls

Appliances.com
Telephone: (888) 543-8345
Fax: (330) 274-2031
Web site: www.appliances.com
Pasta machines and pasta machine motors

Ateco (August Thomsen Corp.)
Telephone: (800) 645-7170
Web site: www.atecousa.com
Nested cookie cutters

Dremel
Telephone: (800) 437-3635
Web site: www.dremel.com
Rotary tool, bits and collets

Golden Artist Colors
Telephone: (800) 959-6543
Web site: www.goldenpaints.com
Iridescent Pearl acrylic paints

The Golden Egg
Telephone: (800) 828-2823
Egg painting stands and tension rods

Hammerhead Adhesives
Telephone: (800) 261-4772
www.hammerheadamerica.com
Two-part epoxy and poster tack

Heart in Hand Studio
Telephone: (702) 243-6564
Web site: www.heartinhandstudio.com
Polymer clay foils, LP polymer clay bonder, compacts, polymer clay texture stamps and purse forms

Hero Arts
Telephone: (800) 822-4376
Web site: www.heroarts.com
Asian Newsprint rubber stamp

Kato Polyclay/Van Aken International
Telephone: (909) 980-2001
Web site: www.katopolyclay.com
Kato Polyclay, Kato Liquid Medium, clay blades and acrylic rollers

Kemper Enterprises
Telephone: (800) 388-5367
Web site: www.kempertools.com
Kemper pattern cutters, ball-tip stylus and needle tools

The Leather Factory
Telephone: (877) 532-8437
Web site: www.leatherfactory.com
Leather stamping tools

Libbey Inc.
Telephone: (888) 794-8469
Web site: www.libbey.com
Square glass votives

Liberty Hardware Mfg. Corp.
Telephone: (800) 542-3789
Web site: www.libertyhardware.com
Key racks

Magenta Rubber Stamps
Telephone: 450-922-5253
Web site: www.magentarubberstamps.com
Floral stamp

The Magnet Source
Telephone: (888) 293-9399
Web site: www.magnetsource.com
Adhesive-backed magnet sheets

Memory Maker Bracelet
Telephone: (800) 746-7666
Web site: www.memorymakerbracelet.com
Photo bracelet frames

National Artcraft Co.
Telephone: (888) 937-2723
Web site: www.nationalartcraft.com
Paintable face watches and clock components

Penn State Industries
Telephone: (800) 377-7297
Web site: www.pennstateind.com
Pen kits and pen assembly press

Penny Black, Inc.
Telephone: (510) 849-1883
Web site: www.pennyblackinc.com
Letter stamp

Polyform Products
Telephone: (847) 427-0020
Web site: www.sculpey.com
Premo Sculpey and Translucent Liquid Sculpey

Polymer Clay Express
Telephone: (800) 844-0138
Web site: www.polymerclayexpress.com
Polymer clay, tools, accessories, related books and videos

Prairie Craft Company
Telephone: (800) 779-0615
Fax: (719) 748-5112
Web site: www.prairiecraft.com
Polymer clay, tools, accessories, books and videos

Ranger Industries, Inc.
Telephone: (800) 244-2211
Web Site: www.rangerink.com
Perfect Pearls, UTEE, pigment stamp pads and Posh Inkabilities metallic inks

Rio Grande
Telephone: (800) 545-6566
Web site: www.riogrande.com
Silver charms, Swarovski crystals, jewelry findings and accessories

Sanford
Telephone: (800) 323-0749
Web site: www.sanfordcorp.com
Prismacolor pencils and Sharpie permanent markers

Scratch-Art Co., Inc.
Telephone: (800) 377-9003
Web site: www.scratchart.com
Shade-Tex rubbing plates

Stamp Oasis
Telephone: (702) 878-6474
Web site: www.stampoasis.com
Rubber stamps and Lacé templates

Toner Plastics
Telephone: (800) 723-1792
Web site: www.tonerplastics.com
Plastic-coated wire

Walnut Hollow
Telephone: (800) 950-5101
Web site: www.walnuthollow.com
Wooden plaques and clock components

Web Sites

Heart in Hand Studio: www.heartinhandstudio.com
Polymer clay related products, classes, workshops and television schedules for Lisa Pavelka.

Polymer Clay Central: www.polymerclaycentral.com
One of the oldest and most comprehensive polymer clay web sites. Filled with project and product information. Great resource for polymer clay links.

Polymer Clay People:
http://groups.yahoo.com/group/Polymer_Clay_People/
A very active newsgroup comprised of hundreds of polymer clay enthusiasts from beginner to professional. This site features online chats with polymer clay artists.

Gallery Artists

Jill Ackiron-Moses
phone: (516) 244-0868
e-mail: jclay33@optonline.net
www.jillackiron-moses.com

Deborah Anderson
phone: (408) 998-5303
e-mail: maraha@aol.com
www.geocities.com/thousand_canes

Judy Belcher
phone: (304) 727-3943
e-mail: jsbel@charter.net

Kim Cavender
phone: (304) 727-6667
e-mail: kjcclay@aol.com

Kathy Davis
phone: (714) 775-8662
e-mail: DAVISNET@earthlink.net

Regina Edmonds
phone: (954) 420-5120
e-mail: fairy111@bellsouth.net
www.pushmolds.com

Rhonda B. Garlick
phone: (702) 648-9253
e-mail: rhondagarlick@cox.net

Samantha Katz
phone: (714) 491-8913
e-mail: samkatz1@earthlink.net

Johnny Kuborssy
phone: (650) 964-4487
e-mail: polypals@aol.com
www.polypals.com

Dotty McMillan
phone: (909) 780-4052
e-mail: dmcmillan01@earthlink.net
www.alookingglass.homestead.com/Dottykaleidoscopes.html

Stephanie Rutz
phone: (702) 362-3393
e-mail: Phanies8@aol.com

Karin Serra
phone: (702) 876-9079
e-mail: serrak@juno.com

Julie Wise
phone: (815) 568-8174
e-mail: wise1J@aol.com
http://members.aol.com/wise1j/page1.html

Irene Yurkewych
phone: (973) 335-3380
e-mail: yurkewych@optonline.net

index

The best in polymer clay projects is from North Light Books!

Polymer Clay Extravaganza

This book features 20 fast, fun and dazzling projects that combine easy polymer clay techniques with a variety of accessible mediums, including mosaic, wire stamping, foiling, mille-fiori, caning and metal embossing. Step-by-step instructions, full-color photos and a section for beginners guarantee success. This unique guide also includes an inspiring idea gallery that encourages crafters to expand their creativity and develop original pieces of their own.

ISBN 1-58180-188-2, paperback, 128 pages, #31960-K

Rubber Stamped Jewelry

Create fabulous jewelry with simple techniques for beautiful results. In no time at all, readers will learn invaluable methods to create lovely earrings, necklaces, bracelets and brooches using a wide array of easy-to-find materials like fabric, paper, polymer clay and, of course, rubber stamps. Guided by easy-to-follow instructions, crafters will find just how easy it is to fashion truly breathtaking and unique jewelry and gifts.

ISBN 1-58180-384-2, paperback, 128 pages, #32415-K

Creative Stamping in Polymer Clay

Filled with fresh designs, simple techniques and gorgeous colors, this exciting book combines two fun, easy-to-master crafts in one. You'll find guidelines for stamping images on all your clay creations, including jewelry, home décor and more, along with advice for experimenting with color and finish. The wide variety of projects guarantees spontaneous, delightful results.

ISBN 1-58180-155-6, paperback, 128 pages, #31904-K

Wild with a Glue Gun

Designed to inspire friends to gather around a table, break out the projects and create with abandon, *Wild with a Glue Gun* offers a stunning array of craft projects, while showing craft clubs and other small groups how to foster an atmosphere of creative sharing.

ISBN 1-58180-472-5, paperback, 144 pages, #32740-K

These and other fine North Light titles are available from your local art & craft retailer, bookstore, online supplier or by calling 1-800-448-0915.